"This book – invaluable to writers – contains essential information about how to protect your work and how to legally use the work of others. The examples, forms, and illustrations really help to make complicated legal concepts easy to understand. At last: a legal guide written by lawyers that tames legalese and brings it within the grasp of the non-lawyer."

—Travis Hunter
Author of *Married But Still Looking* and *The Hearts of Men*

"A highly informative, comprehensive, and easy-to-read legal reference book, the *Literary Law Guide for Authors* is a literary compass for writers who are trying to navigate the confusing maze of information in publishing and intellectual property law."

—Nancey Flowers
Author and managing editor of *QBR The Black Book Review*

"The *Literary Law Guide for Authors* is a well-written, thorough, and straightforward guide that breaks down complicated legal concepts and presents them in a way that the non-lawyer can appreciate. I strongly recommend this book to anyone who needs the basic facts about copyright and trademark law and contracts."

—Ken Shropshire, Esquire
Entertainment lawyer and professor, University of Pennsylvania

"At las[t] analys[...] aspiring [...] information about their legal rights and responsibilities. Our goal has always been to provide writers with the resources necessary for success in the publishing industry. This book is undoubtedly one such resource. It is an invaluable addition to any writer's collection of reference materials."

**—Mack E. Smith and
Sara Freeman Smith**
Authors of *How To Self-Publish & Market Your Book* and owners of WritersHelpDesk.com

"As both an author and an attorney familiar with intellectual property law, I know firsthand what a challenge it is to understand the complex legal issues that arise in writing and publishing. You simply cannot successfully negotiate all the legal requirements and pitfalls in this industry without at least a basic understanding of copyright and contracts, in particular. Thankfully, the *Literary Law Guide for Authors* answers the most common questions, provides real-life examples, and presents complicated information in a delightfully user-friendly way. Therefore, I highly recommend this book to all writers, whether emerging or established; self-published or with a major publishing company."

—Jamellah Ellis, Esquire
Author of *That Faith, That Trust, That Love*

Literary Law Guide for Authors

Copyright, Trademark, and Contracts in Plain Language

Tonya Marie Evans
Susan Borden Evans
Attorneys at Law

Literary Entrepreneur Series™

An imprint of FYOS Entertainment, LLC
Philadelphia

FYOS Entertainment, LLC
ATTN: Permissions Department
PO Box 2021
Philadelphia, PA 19103

LE Series™ Books and logo, FYOS™ and logo, and the title and trade dress of the *Literary Law Guide for Authors* are the intellectual property of FYOS Entertainment, LLC.

Publisher's Cataloging-in-Publication Data

Evans, Tonya Marie.
    Literary law guide for authors : copyright,
  trademark, and contracts in plain language / Tonya Marie
  Evans, Susan Borden Evans.
      p. cm. -- (Literary entrepreneur series)
      Includes bibliographical references and index.
      LCCN 2002092370
      ISBN 0-9674579-6-3

      1. Authors--Legal status, laws, etc.--United States--
  Popular works. 2. Authors and publishers--United States
  --Popular works. 3. Copyright--United States--Popular
  works. 4. Trademarks--United States--Popular works.
  I. Evans, Susan Borden. II. Title.

  KF390.A96E93 2003   343.73'0780705
                             QBI02-200962

Editing by Lisa A. Smith, Writing at Work
Interior design by Rob Roehrick, Roehrick Design
Cover design by James Jones

First Edition

Printed in the United States of America
10 9 8 7 6 5 4 3 2 1

We dedicate this book to the memory and indomitable spirit of William Sutton Borden Sr. (Pop Pop), who endowed us with the same entrepreneurial mind-set that led to the success of countless legendary Borden businesses and with an abiding appreciation of literature and reading.

Contents

Chapter 1

From Writer to Literary Entrepreneur   19

Chapter 2

Copyright   25

Chapter 3

Copyright Registration of Online Works   37

Chapter 4

Other People's Words: Fair Use, Permissions, and Work Made for Hire   41

Foreword

I remember when I first met Tonya and Susan Evans. While attending the 2001 BookExpo America in Chicago, Illinois, I was walking through the Small Press area, as I do every year. Suddenly I heard someone call out, "Mr. Poynter, Mr. Poynter!" I turned to be greeted by Tonya. She introduced herself, escorted me to her booth, and told me about her new publishing company and about how instrumental my book, *The Self-Publishing Manual*, had been for her. At that time I also met her mother, Susan. As we spoke, I marveled at their energy and vision. And I took great pride in meeting yet another family-owned publishing company destined for success.

Tonya and Susan prove that the new publishing model works if you put your plans into motion. That momentum can move you forward to achieve great success in the publishing industry. Tonya and Susan take this momentum even further by using their expertise in intellectual property and publishing law in a new series of law-related guides. The *Literary Law Guide for Authors*, first in the series, contains information desperately needed by authors and publishers alike. Few attorneys devote their practice to publishing law and intellectual property. Fewer still understand the law from the perspectives of attorney, writer, and publisher, as do these dedicated legal eagles.

Like many self-published authors, I fell into publishing. I wrote about what I knew (parachutes) and sold to my friends (skydivers). I was prompted to write *The Self-Publishing Manual* because so many authors wanted to know how to successfully self-publish their work. Tonya and Susan were moved by the same force — a demand for more information — to create this indispensable guidebook.

Since 1969, when I created my publishing company, Para Publishing, I have seen the number of self-published authors increase astronomically. The success of self-published authors, and other independent publishers, has much to do with technological advances that make it more economical to publish in shorter runs. But with all the blessings of self-publishing, not the least of which is creative and business control, come the burdens of managing the legalities of writing.

All too often writers who tend carefully to the creative aspects of their craft do not give the same level of attention to the legal concepts and laws related to it, such as copyright, trademark, constitutional law, and contracts. Whether knowledgeable or not, however, writers are directly affected by these concepts and laws. More than that, writers are responsible for knowing how to protect their work and how to avoid breaking the law in the process. As Tonya and Susan so aptly note, what you don't know about the law as it relates to writing and publishing can hurt you.

The Literary Law Guide for Authors is a timely, well-written, and authoritative layperson's guide to understanding complicated legal concepts. It offers straightforward explanations and relevant examples based on the publishing industry. Most importantly, the fact that lawyers wrote it adds a high level of legitimacy to the information provided.

You will undoubtedly refer to the Literary Law Guide for Authors at every phase of the writing and publishing process. From the chapter on copyright to the valuable forms contained in the appendix and on the companion CD-ROM, each section addresses your most basic and pressing questions in a way that you will easily understand. Tonya and Susan make it possible for you to quickly learn what you need to know about publishing law and intellectual property.

I highly recommend this book to those who want to know more about the legal side of writing. You cannot be a successful author and publisher without effectively traversing the law as it relates to the publishing industry. The Literary Law Guide is your indispensable road map. Happy travels!

Dan Poynter
The Self-Publishing Manual

Preface

Wide-eyed and full of ambition, in 1999 we undertook the task of transforming the raw manuscript of Tonya's poetry into a published book, *Seasons of Her*, which now graces the shelves of bookstores across the country. At first, however, the books, housed in dozens of boxes, graced only the floor of our living room. We quickly discovered that we had a lot to learn about the publishing industry.

Our first step in overcoming a mountain of information was to compile a list of writer's conferences, organizations, Web sites, and magazines (see Appendix A). We found our way to Black Writers Alliance (BWA), Publishers Marketing Association (PMA), and *The Self-Publishing Manual* by Dan Poynter, the guru of independent publishers.

We scoured the pages of *The Self-Publishing Manual* and spent hours surfing the Web sites of various organizations. Quickly we learned that there is strength in numbers, especially when those numbers consist of a network of like-minded people who are open to sharing information and supporting one another. We learned that the BWA was hosting a conference in Atlanta. Without ever laying eyes on any of the members or organizers, but feeling a real sense of camaraderie with her online writer's group, Tonya convinced Susan to buy plane tickets and reserve a hotel room at the conference. Tonya was also invited to perform her poetry at the Friday night poetry event. "What a great way to meet the group in person!" Tonya thought. So on that Friday, we packed our babies (aka our books), checked in for our flight, and checked our baggage (including our babies). We asked the skycap to take good care of them. He said he would. He lied.

Murphy's Law was in full effect on that fateful Friday. A flight delay made us so late we were afraid we would miss the poetry event. We thought that was bad enough. We thought wrong. The worst part was that our babies did not arrive at all that day. Of course anyone who has attended similar conferences knows how important it is to have your books with you to display and sell. So we learned Literary Entrepreneur Rule #1: *never* check your babies.

Luckily, we made it to the poetry event just in time to hear Tonya's name called as the next performer. The next day, Susan had one of those sixth-sense feelings that only mothers have. She decided we should return to the airport to find the lost bag. And there, in the middle of the lost baggage claim area all by itself sat the bag, as if it had been waiting for us all along.

After that experience, we knew things would only get better, and they did. We attended seminars, gathered information, and asked questions; our eyes were opened to a whole new world. We learned the business as writers and publishers from the ground up. We then set out to teach others by using our critical thinking skills and legal knowledge.

That conference changed our lives forever. Established members of the publishing industry taught us information critical to making it in the business. We gathered pages and pages of information that we reviewed, discussed, and condensed into a business plan for our publishing company, FYOS Entertainment, LLC. We had so much to absorb and to prepare for that we didn't mind when our return flight was delayed on the tarmac for hours. We pretended we were on Air Force One planning our next great mission. And we were!

In that planning session, we agreed to embark on an ambitious venture: a series of seminars to educate writers about topics of interest within the publishing industry. Our ultimate goal was to create a group of literary services that would go beyond publishing and that would turn writers into Literary Entrepreneurs. To complete this mission we would capitalize on our unique position as writers, publishers, and attorneys. We turned our plan into action that fall when we partnered with Xlibris (we had met one of their reps at the conference) to co-host our first seminar titled New Technologies in the Literary Industry.

Another step in our mission was to write a series of books for Literary Entrepreneurs. This proved to be a lofty goal because we are so different, and we are, after all, mother and daughter. Tonya, the daughter, is a planner who is organized, detail-oriented, focused, and driven (OK, she's the task-master).

Susan, the mother, is a big-picture person who loves short-term projects with definite deadlines, and she often (read *always*) works up to the very last minute, much to Tonya's chagrin. Thankfully, these differences complement each other wonderfully well. For this first book in the series, Tonya focused on copyright and contracts, Susan concentrated on trademarks, and together they fine-tuned the entire project.

The synergy of opposite energies works because we are both committed to the overall goal of educating Literary Entrepreneurs and, in the process, building a strong family business that will last for years to come. With our seminar series, this book, and our plans for future Literary Entrepreneur Series™ publications, we are well on our way; and so are you.

Symbol Key

When you see this symbol . . .   It means . . .

 Myth: We present, examine, and dispel a common myth.

 Note: We draw your attention to a particular topic of interest.

 Question: We present and answer a frequently asked question.

 Checklist: We list several items to consider on a particular topic.

 Legal Note: We examine the facts and disposition of a leading case, or the status of a statute or pending legislation.

 Contract Clause: We present a key contract clause to be considered.

 Form: We provide the applicable form in Appendix B and on the CD-ROM.

17

 Illustration or Example: We illustrate a particular issue to clarify an important point.

From Writer to
Literary Entrepreneur

Chapter 1

We writers, like other artists and creative people, are notorious for getting caught up in the process of creating, often at the expense of fully comprehending and appreciating the business side of writing. We want to create the next great work of fiction, the most referred to reference guide, the most profound poem, the most telling memoir, the wittiest article or short story or essay. To the writer, mastering the craft of writing in order to complete the manuscript and publish the work is often the sole objective.

These goals, quite obviously, are critical because if we do not nurture and attend to the work during its creation, there is little reason to engage in the process at all. Because of our absorption in the writing, however, little attention is given to the potential legalities we authors face before, during, and after the creative process.

Think for a moment about the countless hours you have already spent (and continue to spend) writing, typing, editing, reading, and critiquing – and writing, typing, editing, reading, and critiquing again. You have undoubtedly attended dozens of writers' conferences; perhaps you've taken writing courses and perused innumerable how-to books on writing, editing, style, and publishing. You have pored over the comments written by family and friends after you've circulated your manuscript for the umpteenth time. And there is no doubt that you have done all of these things with the hope of creating the perfect manuscript, of completing your life-long dream to publish your work.

While you were hunched over your computer or desk writing the next great literary work, did you ever stop to consider the legal implications, rights, and obligations that may exist because of the words you wrote?

When you completed your first novel, poem, or essay, did you stand guard over the stack of pages or the diskette that held your life's passion, forbidding anyone to see your manuscript for fear that they might steal your brilliant ideas? Or worse, did you fall victim to the myth that if you mailed your manuscript to yourself, your copyright interests were somehow protected?

Have you ever mentioned the name of a famous (or not-so-famous but just as real) person in your writing and wondered, if only for a moment, whether it was illegal to do so?

Do you think you should patent the name of your company, trademark your book, and copyright your invention? In other words, are you confused about which term correctly applies to which type of intellectual property and how the three types can, in fact, interrelate under certain circumstances?

Do you hope to sign a publishing contract but lack the knowledge to discuss the basic terms, rights, and obligations with your legal representative, publisher, or agent?

If the answer to any of these questions is yes, then you are reading the right book. This guide gives you the facts about the nature of copyright and trademark, how to protect your intellectual property and other rights, and how to avoid the illegal use of intellectual property belonging to others.

In short, the Literary Law Guide for Authors gives you the information about your legal rights and potential pitfalls in plain language, and provides a comprehensive reference list of other resources. Within these pages you will find real-life examples and illustrations for easy application. In plain language, we present the basic copyright and trademark laws as of the date of publication, basic contract terms, and things to consider before signing on the dotted line. Also, we provide important and necessary forms in this book and on the companion CD. Once you have digested the information here, contact an attorney who specializes in publishing law or intellectual property to see how the general principles we explain may apply to your particular situation. This last bit of advice is most important. Do not use this guide in place of legal counsel by a lawyer knowledgeable in publishing law and intellectual property.

20

The Name Game: Copyright, Trademark, or Patent?

No one word is more misused or more misunderstood by writers than the word "copyright." This single word creates such confusion and lends itself to so much misinformation because rumors, assumptions, and complicated changes in the law make it difficult for writers to separate fact from fiction. But because copyright consists of such a valuable bundle of rights, it is imperative that writers fully comprehend the nature of copyright and the process by which it is protected.

Writers are not the only ones confused by the word "copyright." More than a few business-savvy agents, publishers, and even attorneys, who are in the business of negotiating rights, have a woefully inadequate understanding of the nature of copyright. This is particularly troublesome because writers trust these industry professionals to protect their interests; the explanation that "it's always done this way" is simply not good enough when valuable rights are at stake. So, for you to successfully protect your copyrights and enjoy lucrative financial benefits from successful negotiations to license and sell your rights, you must first understand for yourself how copyright is created and protected.

What you don't know about intellectual property ownership can jeopardize your rights and potentially expose you to legal liability. So let's take a closer look at the differences among the various types of intellectual property.

Copyright: A copyright protects an author's original artistic or literary work, whether published or unpublished. Under copyright law, the term "author" has a special meaning: the creator of an original literary or artistic work. Thus, the word "author" includes not only writers but photographers, singers, painters, sculptors – anyone who creates a literary or artistic work. Examples of literary and artistic works include manuscripts, book covers, song lyrics, sheet music, musical scores, paintings, sketches, sound recordings (music), films, and photographs. And those lists are not all-inclusive.

Trademark: A trademark protects a word, phrase, symbol, or device – the mark – used in business (referred to in the law as commerce) to identify and distinguish one product from another. For example, Striver's Row® is a registered trademark for a series of fiction and nonfiction books on a variety of topics.

Service Mark: A service mark protects a word, phrase, symbol, or device – again, the mark – used in business to identify and distinguish one service from another. For example, e-News Me!℠ is a hypothetical mark referring to the service of providing newsletters, literary services, and seminars.

Patent: The patent is probably the least used intellectual property in the publishing industry. A patent protects an invention by granting the inventor the right to exclude others from producing or using the inventor's discovery or invention for a specific period of time. Some examples of patentable inventions include the talking book, an e-book reader, a typewriter, and an Internet-based customer referral system, such as that used by Amazon.com®.

21

In some instances, patent, copyright, and trademark protection are all available for a single product. For example:

ABC Company has developed a unique method for attaching CDs to the inside back cover of its books; the technique is an advance in the industry. ABC can seek a patent for this novel invention. A copyright exists in the songs on the CD and in the book itself, and those copyrights can be registered. ABC can also seek to register a trademark for this unique book-CD combination, which the company will market as MUSIQUEBOOK™.

An Overview of Literary Law Questions

Authors are, by nature, an inquisitive bunch. Over the years they have asked us many questions about writing and the law. We answer the most important ones in depth in this book. Here's a brief rundown of what you will learn.

What can and cannot be copyrighted? Generally, copyright protects all original writing: letters, e-mail, poetry, fiction, nonfiction, and songs. Book titles cannot be copyrighted. Ideas cannot be copyrighted. As noted earlier, copyright also protects other kinds of creative work, such as photographs, CDs, recordings of written works, musical scores, movies, sculptures, artwork, and even architecture. For more information, see Chapters 2 and 3.

What do you have to do to copyright your work? If you have created an original work in some tangible form – in writing or on film or tape or canvas, for example – then you don't have to do anything. You automatically own your copyright. But you should register it for further protection. For more information, see Chapter 2.

22

How much can you quote without permission? Contrary to popular belief, there is no set number of words you can use under the fair use doctrine. A related question is whether an author needs permission to quote from phone calls, in-person interviews, e-mail, letters, the newspaper, a TV commercial, or a company slogan. The answer will not be satisfying because it is a lawyerly one: it depends. These ever popular questions are dealt with in Chapter 4.

Another often asked question is whether you can use a picture you took of someone else in any way you choose. This question involves balancing the copyright interest in the photograph with the legal concept known as right of publicity. Although the photographer usually owns the copyright in the picture, the person captured in the picture holds a competing interest: the right of publicity. This gives a person the exclusive right to use his or her name, likeness, or other aspect of his or her persona, and the right to prevent others from using those aspects without authorization. For more details, see Chapter 6. Similarly, the photographer may even be prohibited from making and distributing copies of a picture that captures a painting, sculpture, or other work of art if that work is otherwise protected by copyright (see Chapter 4).

Another topic of great concern to writers is writing about real people and real businesses or organizations. Do the same rules apply when you mention your Aunt Tilly as when you mention Oprah? Is the rule the same for writing about the mom-and-pop store on the corner as for McDonald's®? Do the rules change if you say positive things as opposed to negative (but true) things? These questions involve the rights of publicity and privacy and are explored in Chapter 6.

Writers also ask about trademarks and service marks. A common question is: When should the ™ symbol be used, and when is it proper to use the ® symbol? As soon as you have a mark you want to claim trademark rights in, you can use the ™ symbol; you don't need permission to do that. But the ® symbol can be used only after a mark is registered. Authors also want to know about the benefits of trademark registration and whether they can trademark a pen name, character, domain name, or book title. Generally speaking, you cannot trademark a pen name or the title of a single book. But you may be able to register the title of a series of books (e.g., Chicken Soup for the Soul®). For characters, trademark protection depends on whether they are associated with the sale of goods (e.g., Mickey Mouse®). You can also register a domain name if it identifies goods or a service (e.g., Amazon.com®). For more information about these questions and to learn about the difference between common law trademarks, state registered trademarks, and federally registered trademarks, see Chapter 7.

23

Another topic frequently discussed by authors is that of contract negotiations. Specifically, authors ask whether the terms are negotiable. The answer is that despite the commonly held belief perpetuated in the industry, everything is negotiable and should be discussed before you sign on the dotted line. For more information about contracts as well as a discussion of the most important terms and items to consider, see Chapters 12 through 14.

With all of that said, welcome to the complex and often confusing world of literary law. Our goal is to simplify it for you and to help you have a better understanding of your legal rights and responsibilities as a Literary Entrepreneur.

Copyright Chapter 2

Copyright law protects your exclusive right to exploit (use productively) your original work. Copyright law was written to encourage the free exchange of ideas and to stimulate the progress of "useful arts," which benefit society. The theory behind the law is that the progress of useful arts is in the best interest of society but that creative individuals will not freely share their work without some say over how it is used.

The federal Copyright Act provides copyright protection to "authors" (creators) of "original works." The act covers literary, dramatic, musical, artistic, and certain other works of an intellectual nature. Copyright protection is available for both published works (those made available to the public) and unpublished works (those shared with only a few or not at all). To learn more about the history of copyright, see Chapter 10.

Protecting Ideas

The Copyright Act expressly excludes ideas from its protection. *The American Heritage Dictionary* defines "idea" as "something, such as a thought or conception, that potentially or actually exists in the mind as a product of mental activity." Therefore, the *idea* of writing a book about, for instance, a falsely accused prisoner who escapes from jail to prove his innocence and find the real killer cannot be protected under the Copyright Act. But the act does protect a written manuscript based on that idea. This conclusion makes sense in light of the way copyright is created. Copyright protection exists the moment an artistic or literary expression is fixed in a tangible form. Until an idea is *fixed* in a writing or recording, it is just that — an idea. Once fixed in a tangible form, the creative expression (assuming, of course, that it is also original) is protected by copyright.

It is not correct, however, to assume that an idea can never be protected. In fact, the protection of ideas is critical in situations where, for instance, you submit a book proposal to a publisher, pitch a screenplay to a producer or studio, or brainstorm with a collaborator about potential story lines. In such situations, ideas may be protectable under state law related to theories of contract, property, or in some cases, misappropriation.

25

When Copyright Ownership Begins

Copyright exists *automatically* when the work is created. For the purposes of copyright law, a work is created when it is fixed in a copy or phonorecord for the first time. By "copy" the law means material objects, such as books, manuscripts, electronic files, Web sites, e-mail, sheet music, musical scores, film, videotape, or microfilm, from which a work can be read or visually perceived either directly or with the aid of a machine or device. Phonorecords are material objects, such as cassette tapes, CDs, or LPs – but not motion picture soundtracks on which sounds are recorded and which combine moving images and sound. Thus, for example, a song (the work) can be fixed in sheet music (copies) or in a CD (phonorecord) or both. If a work is created over a period of time, the copyright applies automatically to whatever part is fixed on a particular date. So as soon as you write the first two paragraphs of your book, whether by hand on paper or by keying them into a computer, those paragraphs are immediately and automatically copyrighted – even if you don't get around to writing the third paragraph until a week or a year later.

Copyright protection is not available for any work of the United States government (for example, any publication created by a governmental agency, like the Copyright Office), but the United States government may receive and hold copyrights transferred to it by assignment, bequest, or otherwise.

Showing the World That You Own Your Work

To demonstrate to the world that you own your work, you should use a copyright notice. The notice should contain all of the following three elements:

- ☞ **The symbol,** which for printed material is the letter "C" in a circle – ©; or, for CDs, audio tapes, and LPs, the letter "P" in a circle – ℗. Instead of the symbol you may use the word "Copyright" or the abbreviation "Copr."

- ☞ **The year** in which the work is first published. If your work is a compilation or a derivative that includes previously published material, use the year in which you first publish it. If your work consists of a picture, graphic, or sculpture, with or without accompanying text, and it is reproduced on greeting cards, postcards, stationery, jewelry, dolls, toys, or any useful article, no date is necessary.

- ☞ **The name** of the copyright owner. (If you're writing under a pseudonym, see page 49.)

The copyright statement would then look like this: © **2003 Patsi Pen.**

You should also consider including the phrase "All rights reserved." This phrase lets the public know that you have reserved each right in the bundle of rights that copyright contains. In that case, the copyright statement would look like this: © **2003 Patsi Pen. All rights reserved.**

Although use of the copyright notice is no longer required by law, it is still important that it appear in all copyrighted works because it informs the public that the work is protected by copyright, identifies the copyright owner, and shows the year of first publication. Copyright notice is still required by law, however, for works that were published before 1989 (see Chapter 10). Furthermore, if your copyright is infringed, and a proper notice of copyright appears on the published copy to which the infringer had access, then he or she cannot argue that the infringement was innocent. Innocent infringement can occur only when the infringer did not realize that the work was protected. (See Chapter 5.)

 The copyright owner has the responsibility to use the copyright notice and doesn't need anyone's permission to use it. The copyright owner can use the notice without registering with the Copyright Office.

What a Copyright Owner Has the Right to Do

In general, the Copyright Act gives a copyright owner the exclusive right to do and to authorize others to do the following:

- ☑ **Reproduce** the work (make copies)

- ☑ **Prepare derivative works** based on the original (create a motion picture based on a novel or a novel based on a motion picture)

- ☑ **Distribute copies** of the work to the public (publish) by sale or other transfer of ownership, or by rental, lease, or lending

- ☑ **Perform the work publicly** (a public reading)

- ☑ **Display the work publicly** (hang a painting in an art gallery)

- ☑ **Perform the work publicly by means of a digital audio transmission (DAT)**, in the case of sound recordings

Collectively, these rights are often referred to as an author's exclusive bundle of rights.

| ???? | Without the copyright symbol on my manuscript, I won't have any copyright protection. |

This is false. In 1989, the United States joined the Berne Convention for the Protection of Literary and Artistic Works, which is an international copyright treaty that requires all member countries to eliminate formal requirements as a condition to copyright protection. As a result, you *do not* have to use the copyright symbol or notice, or even register your copyright with the Copyright Office in order to create a protectable copyright interest. Copyright in original works of authorship exists as soon as the work is fixed in a tangible form.

Scope of Copyright Protection

The Copyright Act protects only original works fixed in a tangible medium of expression now known or later developed, from which they can be perceived, reproduced, or otherwise communicated, either directly or with the aid of a machine or device. Works of authorship include the following categories:

- ☑ Literary works
- ☑ Musical works, including any accompanying words
- ☑ Dramatic works, including any accompanying music
- ☑ Pantomimes and choreographic works
- ☑ Pictorial, graphic, and sculptural works
- ☑ Motion pictures and other audiovisual works
- ☑ Sound recordings
- ☑ Architectural works

The Elements of Copyrightable Works

Originality: Copyrightable works must be original; that is, the work (story, song, poem, drawing, movie, and so forth) must be of the author's own creation. The originality requirement has a low threshold and *does not* require novelty, ingenuity, or any particular quality.

Fixation: An author's creation must be fixed in a tangible medium of expression. For instance, copyright does not exist until a story is written, typed, or recorded. The fixation may be viewed by way of a machine such as a computer, projector, digital camera, scanner, or even a machine that has not yet been created. But an idea, procedure, process, system, method of operation, concept, principle, or discovery is not protectable by copyright. Also, a live performance that is not fixed in a tangible form (written or recorded) is not protected by copyright law. Simultaneous fixation, such as a live broadcast of a sporting event, is protected by copyright.

> **?** Neo Pro, Inc., hosts a weekly performance as part of its Neo Pro Performance Series℠. At these neosoul performances, the renowned poet Flow performs original live poetry from her book *Flow's Show* with a live band, which was previously recorded by her producer, Mr. Soul Explosion. Has a copyright been created in Flow's poetry? In Mr. Soul Explosion's music? How does the live performance factor into the equation?
>
> **Answer:** Flow's poetry is copyrighted because it is both *original* and *fixed* as a writing in her book. The music of Mr. Soul Explosion is copyrighted because it is *original* and previously recorded, thus *fixed* in a tangible expression. Additionally, both Flow and Mr. Soul Explosion have the right to engage in the live performance of their copyrighted work.

Copyright Registration

Registration of your copyright creates a public record of the facts and circumstances pertaining to it. While registration is *not* necessary for copyright protection, the Copyright Act gives you certain advantages under the law if you do register your work.

> The Copyright Office ordinarily does not compare copyright registration forms with existing deposit copies or registration records to determine whether works submitted for registration are similar to any material for which a registration of a copyright claim already exists. Therefore, the records of the Copyright Office may contain any number of registrations for works describing or illustrating the same underlying idea, method, or system.

29

Advantages of Copyright Registration

☑ You can file an infringement suit only if the copyright is registered.

☑ If made before or within five years of publication, registration establishes sufficient (*prima facie*) evidence in court of the validity of the copyright and of the facts stated in the registration certificate.

☑ If you register within three months after publication of the work or prior to an infringement, the defendant is required to prove that infringement does not exist. This is a critical advantage because ordinarily the person who files a lawsuit has to prove his or her case; but if you have registered your copyright in a timely manner, then the burden of proof falls to the defendant.

☑ If registration is made within three months after publication of the work or prior to an infringement, statutory damages and attorney's fees will be available to the copyright owner in court actions. Otherwise, only an award of actual damages and profits is available.

☑ Registration allows the copyright owner to record the registration with the U. S. Customs Service for protection against the importation of infringing copies.

? As a U.S. citizen, can I protect my copyright outside of the United States?

Answer: There is no such thing as an international copyright that will protect your work in every country. Each country has its own copyright laws. Nonetheless, most countries do offer foreign works some protection against infringement based in large part on certain international treaties and conventions (see Chapter 10).

How to Register: For the original registration of your book, manuscript, poetry, other text, or other artistic work, send an application form, a non-refundable filing fee ($30 as of this writing) for each application, and one or more nonreturnable samples of the work being registered to the Copyright Office. All three items should be submitted in the same package; an incomplete submission will not be processed and may be returned. You can contact the Copyright Office for specific deposit requirements, which means how many and what kind of physical copies of your particular work the Copyright Office will require for review. Deposit requirements vary according to the type of work and the publication status. For contact information, see page 36 at the end of this chapter.

To track your copyright application materials, send all correspondence via certified or registered mail, and request a return receipt; or send via an overnight service. Also, never send the only copy of your work.

[????] If I mail my manuscript to myself that is as good as registering my copyright with the Library of Congress.

This myth is known as the poor man's copyright, but it does not offer any additional protection beyond that which already exists once your idea is fixed and thus your work is created. Also it does not constitute a registration of your copyright.

Types of Application Forms: The following application forms, which are the most relevant types for writers, are all reproduced in Appendix B and on the CD-ROM:

Form TX for published and unpublished nondramatic literary works

Form PA 🗎 for published and unpublished works of the performing arts (musical and dramatic works, pantomimes and choreographic works, motion pictures and other audiovisual works)

Form SE 🗎 for serials, works issued or intended to be issued in successive parts bearing numerical or chronological designations (Issue 1, 2, 3, etc. or Fall Issue, Spring Issue, etc.) and intended to be continued indefinitely (periodicals, newspapers, magazines, newsletters, annuals, journals, etc.)

Form SR 🗎 for published and unpublished sound recordings

Form VA 🗎 for published and unpublished works of the visual arts (pictorial, graphic, and sculptural works, including architectural works)

Effective Date: Copyright registration is effective on the date the Copyright Office receives all of the required elements in acceptable form.

Evidence of Application and Registration: If you apply for copyright registration, you will not receive an acknowledgment that your application has been received because the Copyright Office receives more than six hundred thousand applications each year. However, a Copyright Office staff member will call or send a letter if further information is needed. You will receive a certificate of registration indicating that the work has been registered, or, if the application cannot be accepted, a letter explaining why it has been rejected.

Correcting an Error in the Original Application: To correct an error in a copyright registration or to add information, you must file a supplementary registration form – Form CA 🗎 – with the Copyright Office. The current filing fee for Form CA is $100.

How to Investigate the Copyright Status of a Work

31

There are several ways to investigate whether a work is protected by copyright or whether it is in the public domain. The easiest way to begin is to examine the work for the copyright notice information, place and date of publication, and author information. The second way is to conduct a search of the Copyright Office catalog and other records. The third way is to have the Copyright Office conduct a search for you.

The Copyright Office published the *Catalog of Copyright Entries* (*CCE*) in book form from 1891 to 1978 and in microfiche form from 1979 to 1982. Many libraries maintain copies of the *CCE*, and the *CCE* may be a good starting point for research. Because the *CCE* does not contain copyright assignment and other recorded documents, however, it cannot be the only method used to track copyright ownership conclusively. Also, while the *CCE* includes facts about copyright registration, it does not provide a verbatim account nor does it include contact information for the copyright claimant. Copyright registrations after 1978 are found online only, in the Copyright Office database.

Where to Search for Information about Registered Copyrights

The Copyright Office is in the Library of Congress James Madison Memorial Building, 101 Independence Avenue, S.E., Washington, D.C. 20559-6000. Most Copyright Office records are open to public inspection and searching from 8:30 A.M. to 5:00 P.M. Eastern time, Monday through Friday, except federal holidays. The general public can conduct free searches of the card catalog, the automated catalog containing records from 1978 forward, record books, and microfilm records of assignments and related documents. Certain records, including correspondence files and deposit copies, can be accessed only by paying a $75 per hour search fee. You will find the Copyright Office fee schedule in Appendix B and on the CD-ROM. Be advised, however, that fees are subject to change; you can verify the actual amount of search fees at www.copyright.gov.

The Copyright Office staff will search its records for you for a fee of $75 per hour. Based on the initial information you furnish, the office will provide an estimate of the total search fee, which you submit along with your request. The office will then proceed with the search and send you a typewritten report or, if you prefer, an oral report by telephone. In the case of search requests based on evidentiary requirements for a lawsuit, search reports can be certified on request for an extra fee of $80 per hour. Note that the search fee does not include the cost of additional certificates, photocopies of deposits, or copies of other Copyright Office records.

Transfer of Copyright

Any or all of the copyright owner's bundle of rights or any subdivision of those rights may be transferred to a third party. A transfer is defined in Section 101 of the Copyright Act as an assignment, mortgage, grant of an exclusive license, transfer by will or intestate succession, or any other change in the ownership of any or all of the exclusive rights in a copyright whether or not it is limited in time or place of effect.

Generally, there are three types of transfers: a nonexclusive license, an exclusive license, and an assignment. Further limits on transfer include the number of rights transferred, the term, and the geographical scope. To be valid, the transfer of exclusive rights must be in a written agreement signed by the owner of the rights conveyed (or the owner's authorized agent). But nonexclusive transfer of a right does not require a written agreement. So for example, the transfer of the exclusive right of publication to a publisher or agent requires a signed agreement, but the transfer of the nonexclusive right to reproduce an excerpt of a literary work in a newsletter does not.

As a matter of course, however, you should get into the habit of writing all agreements relating to your copyright interests. Having a signed agreement memorializes the terms and reduces the likelihood of misunderstandings as to what was promised by each party. (See Chapter 12 for more information about contracts).

A copyright may also be transferred by operation of law. For instance, copyright can be bequeathed by will, or by state law if an individual dies without a will. Copyright is a personal property right, and it is subject to the various state laws and regulations that govern the ownership, inheritance, or transfer of personal property and the terms of contracts or conduct of business. For information about relevant state laws, consult an attorney in your area.

Copyright assignments can be recorded in the Copyright Office as transfers of copyright ownership. Recording the assignment gives notice to the world that the copyright interest has been transferred. Although you are not required to record the transfer to make it valid, recording the assignment does provide certain legal advantages and may be required to validate the transfer against third parties. For instance, under certain conditions, recordation establishes the order of priority between conflicting transfers (that is, who received the transfer first), or between a conflicting transfer and a nonexclusive license. Recordation also establishes a public record of the transaction and provides "constructive notice," which is a legal term meaning that members of the public are deemed to have been notified even if they have not actually received notice of the transfer. To establish constructive notice, the recorded document must describe the work with specificity so that it could be identified by a reasonable search, and the work must be registered with the Copyright Office.

33

Reclaiming Your Copyright after Transfer

Did you know that regardless of the terms of your transfer document (a publishing agreement, license, or so forth), you have the right to reclaim your copyright? Discussion about this little known legal right for authors is all but nonexistent in the publishing industry, and for obvious reasons. Publishers, for instance, may not want authors to know that the "life of copyright" term in most publishing agreements can be rendered null and void if a statutory termination is properly effected.

Section 203 of the Copyright Act provides that a transfer or license of copyright (or any right in the bundle of rights) executed by the author on or after January 1, 1978, is subject to termination under the following conditions:

☑ A single author who executed a grant may terminate it. If the author is deceased, then whoever is entitled to exercise more than one-half of that author's rights may terminate it.

☑ If two or more authors executed a grant of a joint work, a majority of the authors who executed it may terminate it. If any of the joint authors is dead, his or her termination interest may be exercised by whoever is entitled to exercise more than one-half of that author's interest.

This single, extremely valuable section of the Copyright Act empowers authors.

Note that the statutory termination provision does not apply to works made for hire or to transfers made by will. The termination right also does not apply to rights arising under foreign laws or derivative works. In the case of derivative works (for example, a movie based on a book), termination of the rights to the underlying work (the book) does not prevent the continued display and distribution of the derivative movie. Once the rights are terminated, however, no new derivative works can be created.

Not surprisingly, the rules to exercise the statutory termination right are specific and must be strictly adhered to or the right will be forever lost.

First, termination can be effected only during a five-year window of opportunity. For works transferred before January 1, 1978, the window begins either fifty-six years after the date the copyright was originally secured or on January 1, 1978, whichever is later. For works transferred on or after January 1, 1978, the window begins thirty-five years after the grant was made. Special rules apply if the right transferred is the right of publication. In that case, the window

34

begins thirty-five years from the date of publication or at the end of forty years from the date the transfer was executed, whichever is earlier. Presumably this modification accounts for the gap in time between the date a publishing agreement is signed and the date the work is actually published.

Second, the current owner must deliver to the grantee a signed, written, advance termination notice, which includes the effective date of termination, not less than two years or more than ten years before the termination is to take effect. The notice must be in writing, declare the effective date of termination, and be signed by the owner (or owners, as per the statute) or a duly authorized agent, who may be an attorney-in-fact under a power of attorney, or, if the owner is deceased, an heir or beneficiary under a will. The notice must be recorded with the Copyright Office *before* the termination is to take place, and the underlying work must be registered with the Copyright Office.

Third, the Copyright Act states, "Termination of the grant may be effected *notwithstanding any agreement to the contrary . . .*" Therefore, you cannot "contract around" this right. In other words, you cannot waive these rights by contract. Your right to terminate exists until it is exercised or lost, pursuant to the terms of the statute.

> Let's bring this topic home by way of example. Assume that Author, at age 30, signs a publishing agreement with XYZ Publisher on January 1, 2003. In that agreement, Author transfers to XYZ the right to publish in hardback and paperback and all subsidiary rights (see Chapter 13). The work is published eighteen months later, on July 1, 2004. On January 1, 2010, XYZ licenses the right to develop a motion picture based on the book.
>
> Because the transferring contract was signed on January, 1, 2003, before the publication date, the five-year window springs into effect thirty-five years later, on January, 1, 2038, and ends on January 1, 2043. During that window, Author has the right to terminate the agreement and reclaim all rights transferred to Publisher. If Author intends to terminate the publishing agreement on the first date the window comes into effect, she will have to send a termination notice to the Publisher or his assignee no earlier than January 1, 2028, and no later than January 1, 2036. Once the transfer terminates, Publisher can no longer create any derivative works or license that right to others.

It is crucial to understand when the termination window exists and to plan properly to reclaim your rights. Additionally, you should plan for the reclamation of your rights in your will so that your family, executor, or trustee knows that your intellectual property exists and understands how to manage and protect those rights after your death. This, of course, means that you must consult a trust and estates attorney familiar with intellectual property laws to create an estate plan that includes a will and perhaps a trust, financial power of attorney, and healthcare power of attorney with a medical directive (aka a living will), so that you protect not only your personal property and real estate but also your intellectual property. In particular, consider creating a testamentary trust in your will to name a literary trustee knowledgeable about intellectual property to maintain and administer your intellectual property rights after your death. This is a special type of trustee who will probably be someone other than one whom you would usually name because the literary trustee should be familiar with intellectual property law. (See "The Role of a Literary Trustee," a feature article by Ed McCoyd, in the August 2002 issue of *Author's Guild Bulletin.*)

Copyright Office Contact Information

☑ Mailing address: Library of Congress
Copyright Office
101 Independence Avenue, S.E.
Washington, D.C. 20559-6000

☑ Internet address: www.copyright.gov

☑ Public Information Office (live and recorded information): 202-707-3000 (8:30 A.M. to 5:00 P.M. Eastern Time), Monday through Friday, except federal holidays

☑ Forms and Publications Hotline: 202-707-9100 (24 hours a day, 7 days a week). Request application forms and informational circulars by name or number. If you are unsure which form or circular to order, call the Public Information Office instead.

☑ Fax-on-Demand: 202-707-2600 (24 hours a day, 7 days a week). Use only to request informational circulars. Application forms are not available by fax but can be downloaded at the Web site.

☑ TTY: 202-707-6737. For the hearing impaired. Messages may be left on the TTY line 24 hours a day. Calls are returned between 8:30 A.M. and 5:00 P.M. Eastern time, Monday through Friday, except federal holidays.

Copyright Registration
of Online Works
Chapter 3

The question often arises as to how the Copyright Act applies to online works. The Internet and other technological advances certainly do present numerous challenges to existing copyright law. But an online work is no different from its physical counterpart, except for the way the information is viewed or perceived. Therefore, there is no one form used specifically to register online works. In fact, the Copyright Office advises that the forms TX, PA, VA, and SR are mainly for office administrative purposes and therefore, technically, a work may be registered on any form.

Of course you should try to use the form most appropriate for your particular situation, and this decision depends on the nature of the online work you want to register. Here are some guidelines to help you choose the proper form:

- ☑ Form TX 🗐 – if the text predominates, and there are few or no images or sounds appearing in the work

- ☑ Form VA 🗐 – if the pictures or graphics predominate the work, even if there are accompanying words

- ☑ Form PA 🗐 – if audiovisual material (sound connected to images, like an online video) predominates

- ☑ Form SR 🗐 – if sounds predominate (except the sounds that accompany and are intrinsic to an audiovisual work)

Also consider that some Web sites can be considered serials (recurring regularly, like a weekly e-newsletter or e-bulletin). In that case, the following forms should be considered:

- ☑ Form SE 🗐 – for a single issue of a serial

- ☑ Form SE/GROUP 🗐 – for a group of issues of a serial, including daily newsletters

- ☑ Form GR/CP– for a group of contributions to a periodical, and used in conjunction with Form TX, PA, or VA

Your registration form should refer only to copyrightable information that is clearly identified in the form, has not been previously registered or published, and is not in the public domain. For published online works, the registration form should include only the content of the work actually published on the date given on the application.

Revisions and Updates

Problems of registration arise when a Web site is updated frequently. The question is whether it is necessary to register the site after each update. For individual works the answer, technically, is yes, because there is no comprehensive registration to cover revisions published on different dates. Therefore, each daily update would have to be registered separately. As attorneys we recommend that you do register each update to be fully protected. We recognize, however, that this would require much work, and we acknowledge that most people don't follow this practice because they find it to be impractical. If you are like most people, then we suggest that you make it a practice to register your Web site every three months. If you do that, then you will be entitled to statutory damages and attorney fees if you ever have to sue someone for infringement. A different rule governs automated databases and serials because they qualify to use blanket registration (see below).

Automated Databases

Some frequently updated online works, like Amazon.com®, are considered automated databases, because the Web site consists of facts, data, and other pre-existing information organized in files for retrieval by means of a computer. When that is so, a group of updates to the database, whether published or unpublished, that cover up to three months within the same calendar year may be combined in a single, blanket registration. For more information about online databases, review Copyright Office Circular 65.

E-Newsletters and Other E-Serials

Group registration is defined by the Copyright Office as a single registration covering multiple issues published on different dates. Group registration is available for works published weekly or less often (serials) and for newsletters published daily or more often than weekly, including those published online. The requirements vary, depending on the type of work. See Copyright Office Circular 62 for more information on serials. Note that group registration is only available for collective works, which include a collection of articles, and not for electronic journals published one article at a time.

What Samples of Online Works to Send to the Copyright Office

For online works, the Copyright Office requires a deposit of one of the following:

Option A: A computer disk, labeled with the name of the title and author, that contains the entire work, and a representative portion of the work in a format such as a printout, audiocassette, or videotape that can be reviewed by the Copyright Office. If the work is five pages or less of text or artwork, or three minutes or less of music, sounds, or audiovisual material, send the entire work as the deposit and note that it is complete. If the work is longer than that, deposit five representative pages or three representative minutes.

Option B: A reproduction of the entire work, regardless of length, in the format appropriate for the work being registered. For example, send a printout of a Web site made up of text or images, an audio-cassette of sounds, or a videotape of audiovisual material. With this option, no computer disk is required.

These options apply when the work appears *online only*. If a work is published both online (for example, at the creator's Web site) and by the distribution of physical copies (an author's book, an artist's poster) in any format, then you must follow the regulations for depositing the copies.

For computer programs, databases, and works fixed in CD-ROM format transmitted online, the Copyright Office provides some guidance in Circulars 61 and 65. The office defines a computer program as "a set of statements or instructions to be used directly or indirectly in a computer in order to bring about a certain result." Deposit requirements for computer programs vary according to whether or not the work contains trade secrets. Trade secrets are defined by legal treatises as "any information that can be used in the operation of a business or other enterprise and that is sufficiently valuable and secret to afford an actual or potential economic advantage over others." If your work contains trade secrets, then you should include a cover letter stating that it does, along with the page containing the copyright notice, if any, and one of the following:

For entirely new computer programs

☑ The first and last twenty-five pages of source code with portions containing trade secrets blocked out

☑ The first and last ten pages of source code alone, with no blocked-out portions

☑ The first and last twenty-five pages of object code plus any ten or more consecutive pages of source code, with no blocked-out portions

☑ For programs fifty pages or less in length, the entire source code with trade secret portions blocked out

For revised computer programs

☑ If revisions are present in the first and last twenty-five pages, any one of the four options above, as appropriate

☑ If revisions are not present in the first and last twenty-five pages, twenty pages of source code containing the revisions with no blocked-out portions, or any fifty pages of source code containing the revisions with some portions blocked out

For automated databases, the deposit requirements are as follows:

☑ For a single-file database (which contains data records pertaining to a single common subject matter) you must deposit the first and last twenty-five pages or, under a grant of special relief if you do not want to disclose trade secrets, the first and last twenty-five data records.

☑ For multiple-file databases (which contain separate and distinct groups of data records), you must deposit the first fifty data records from each file, or the entire file, whichever is less, or fifty pages or data records total under a grant of special relief. Also, you must include a descriptive statement that includes the title of the database; the name and address of copyright claimant; and the name and content of each separate file within the database, including subject matter, origin of data, and number of separate records within each file. For published multiple-file databases, also include a description and sample of the exact contents of any copyright notice used in or with the database (plus manner and frequency of display).

☑ For a revised database (either single or multiple file), you must deposit fifty pages or records showing the revisions, or the entire revised portions if less than fifty pages.

For works fixed in CD-ROM format, deposit one complete copy of the CD-ROM, including any operating software or instruction manual, if applicable.

Other People's Words:
Fair Use, Permissions, and
Work Made for Hire

Chapter 4

Writers frequently want to quote from works written by others. Writers and publishers engage the services of editors, indexers, and others who may change or add words in the process of helping to create a finished work. What does the Copyright Act say in regard to such use of words written by others?

Fair Use

The doctrine of fair use significantly limits copyright protection. This doctrine permits use of copyrighted materials for certain purposes listed in the Copyright Act, such as criticism, comment, news reporting, teaching (including multiple copies for classroom use), scholarship, or research. While technically infringing on the copyright owner's rights, these uses are considered permissible; and such fair use can be used as a defense against a claim of copyright infringement.

Unfortunately, the proper application of fair use is at best difficult to determine. Contrary to popular belief, there is no specific number of words, lines, or notes of a copyrighted work that may safely be used without permission. Also, it is not sufficient simply to acknowledge the source of the copyrighted material. If your use is not fair use (and if no other exception, such as those explained in Chapter 5, applies), you must obtain permission.

[????] A certain number of words of copyrighted material can be used without the permission of the owner.

This myth among writers that using, say, 500 words or less of any copyrighted material is always fair use is just that: a myth. It is not true. In fact, copyright law does not set a precise amount of a copyrighted work that can be used without the owner's permission. The Copyright Act provides a series of factors to be considered to determine whether fair use exists.

How to Establish Fair Use

The Copyright Act provides four factors to determine, on a case-by-case basis, whether fair use or infringement exists.

☑ **Character or Purpose of Use:** Allowable use includes criticism (reviews), comment (reviews), news reporting, teaching (classroom), scholarship (reference materials), research (law review articles), and parody (as in the book *The Wind Done Gone*, by Alice Randall). Note that use for commercial purposes will not automatically preclude a finding of fair use. Therefore, selling a book of movie reviews does not, in itself, defeat a fair use argument.

☑ **Nature of Copyrighted Work:** A court takes into consideration the type of work involved — for example, whether it is fiction or non-fiction, published or unpublished. Jonathan Kirsch, author of *Kirsch's Handbook of Publishing Law*, states that in general a court is less likely to find fair use when a work of fiction or fantasy is copied than one dealing with facts and figures, or when the work is unpublished or consists of private letters.

☑ **Amount and Substantiality of the Copied Work:** Although no set number of words determines fair use, a court will consider how much of the copyrighted work was used (in other words, did you use one word or a few words, or did you use a large portion of the whole work). Infringement can be found, however, even when only a few words are used if those words are the heart of the copyrighted work.

☑ **Effect on the Potential Market:** A court will ask whether use of the copyrighted work lessens the value of that work. If the use harms the copyright owner's ability to benefit financially from the copyrighted work, it is less likely that fair use exists. If, however, the quoted material is properly credited to the owner and that credit increases the likelihood of sales for the owner, then it is more likely that fair use exists.

Unfortunately, applying these four factors often raises more questions than it answers, and even a comprehensive analysis of the factors provides no absolute conclusions. Only a judge can make the ultimate decision as to whether a particular use is fair.

The Impact of New Technologies on Fair Use Analysis: The fair use doctrine was created in a time when the main mode of transmitting creative works was in print form. With new technologies that allow one person to store large amounts of information in digital form and transmit that same information in perfect condition to millions of people with a few clicks of the mouse, it is easy (and scary) to imagine the innumerable infringements of copyrighted work that exist every second of every day and that remain unpoliced and incapable of control. In light of this twenty-first century reality, some scholars believe that the law lags far behind in closing the gap between yesterday's statutes and tomorrow's technology.

Getting Permission to Use the Work of Others

To acquire permission from a copyright owner to use his or her copyrighted work in, for instance, your manuscript, you must use a permissions request. Perhaps you want to include a quotation or excerpt from another author's copyrighted work, or a photograph or an illustration, and your use would not be considered fair use (and we have already discussed how difficult it is to determine whether fair use exists). In that case, or even if fair use clearly exists, you may consider getting permission in writing. Also, when you sign a publishing agreement you will often be required to obtain any necessary written permissions to use copyrighted material because the publisher does not want to be exposed to legal liability for infringement.

A permissions request should

- ☑ describe the copyrighted material with great specificity
- ☑ note the source of the material
- ☑ state whether the material has been previously published and, if so, state the date, author, publisher, and current owner
- ☑ include a grant of permission that specifically states how the material can be used, including any limitations on use (if applicable)
- ☑ state whether the grant is exclusive or nonexclusive (and if nonexclusive, whether it is revocable or irrevocable)
- ☑ include specifications for copyright notice and credit
- ☑ include a declaration of control in which the owner expressly states that he or she is the sole owner and has the power to give the requested permission, or if not the sole owner, whom you should contact to get the necessary signatures from the other owners. As a matter of efficiency, you should try to get all owners to sign off on the same permission form.

Finding out how to reach the person who has the authority to grant permission to use pictures, quotes, and other copyrighted work can be difficult. Here are some possibilities:

- ☑ Copyright and permissions request information is listed on the back of the title page in most books.
- ☑ Copyright Clearance Center, Inc. (CCC) – www.copyright.com (not to be confused with the unrelated Copyright Office at www.copyright.gov). Contact CCC if the work is part of a book or a journal article. CCC is a licensor of text reproduction rights.

43

☑ National Writers Union (NWU) – An organization representing free-lance writers in American markets. Contact NWU for permissions to use articles by freelance writers via the Publication Rights Clearinghouse: prc@nwu.org.

☑ Harry Fox Agency – HFA (National Music Publisher's Association) is a licensor of musical works. Contact HFA at http://www.nmpa.org/contact.html or 711 Third Avenue, New York, NY 10017. Telephone: 212-370-5330, Fax: 212-953-2384: Los Angeles: 323-466-3861: Nashville: 615-242-4173, clientrelations@harryfox.com.

☑ ASCAP – The American Society of Composers, Authors and Publishers is a performing rights organization. Find songwriters, composers, and publishers at www.ascap.com. Licensor of public performance rights as follows:

- Internet licensing: weblicense@ascap.com

- Cable or satellite licensing: cablelicensing@ascap.com

- Television licensing: TVLicensing@ascap.com

- Radio licensing: radiolicensing@ascap.com

- General licensing: licensing@ascap.com

☑ BMI – Broadcast Music, Inc., is a performing rights organization. Find songwriters, composers, and publishers at www.bmi.com. Licensor of public performance rights as follows:

- Internet licensing: weblicensing@bmi.com

- TV, radio, and cable: licensing@bmi.com

- General licensing: genlic@bmi.com

☑ SESAC – The Society of European Stage Authors and Composers is a performing rights organization. Find songwriters, composers, and publishers at www.sesac.com. Licensor of public performance rights in the United States:

- Pat Collins, senior vice president – pcollins@sesac.com

- Maxine Edwards, director, administration/support – medwards@sesac.com

- Deborah Houghton, vice president, broadcast licensing – dhoughton@sesac.com

- Bill Lee, vice president, licensing operations – blee@sesac.com

- Greg Riggle, associate director, broadcast licensing – griggle@sesac.com

☞ Icopyright.com – Online licensor of digital content (work published on the Internet) – www.icopyright.com.

☞ The Photographer's Index – Connect with owners of photographic works at www.photographersindex.com.

Work Made for Hire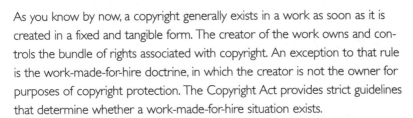

As you know by now, a copyright generally exists in a work as soon as it is created in a fixed and tangible form. The creator of the work owns and controls the bundle of rights associated with copyright. An exception to that rule is the work-made-for-hire doctrine, in which the creator is not the owner for purposes of copyright protection. The Copyright Act provides strict guidelines that determine whether a work-made-for-hire situation exists.

Work made for hire can occur in two contexts: that involving employers and employees and that involving independent contractors. In the first, work made for hire is done by employees within the scope of their employment. In the second, an independent contractor is specially commissioned to perform work for one of the following purposes only:

☑ a contribution to a collective work

☑ a part of a motion picture or other audiovisual work

☑ a translation

☑ a supplementary work, which includes such things as forewords, editorial changes, and indexes

☑ a compilation

☑ an instructional text

☑ a test

☑ answer material for a test

☑ a sound recording

☑ an atlas

Furthermore, the work performed by the independent contractor is considered to be work made for hire only if the contractor and the hiring person both sign a contract *before* the work begins stating that the work is made for hire.

Because the existence of work made for hire depends on the relationship of the parties involved, the first question to answer is whether the creator is an employee or an independent contractor.

45

Employee: In the employer/employee relationship, the employer controls the work product, work site, work schedule, and assignments; provides the equipment used to perform the work; pays the employee a regular salary and takes appropriate deductions; and so forth. For example, a staff writer is an employee of a newspaper company. In that situation, the newspaper company and not the staff writer owns the copyright of all work produced by the writer during his employment.

Independent contractor: Unlike employees, independent contractors maintain control over how the work they do is done. Independent contractors are in business for themselves. They provide their own equipment, and set their own hours and work schedule. They may refer to themselves as business owners, freelancers, self-employed, or consultants. They are their own bosses.

If you want an independent contractor to contribute to your product, and you want to retain copyright to his or her contribution, then as stated earlier you must both sign a work-made-for-hire agreement before the work begins. You will find a sample agreement in Appendix B, but here's a checklist of important items that should be included in any work-made-for-hire agreement:

- ☑ the name, type of entity (corp., LLC, etc.), and address of each party
- ☑ a paragraph that sets forth the complete description of the work and the amount of compensation involved
- ☑ a list of all rights included, which should be the entire bundle of rights
- ☑ a statement that the creator has no rights in the work created or in the work in which the creation is used
- ☑ an assignment provision that assigns all rights, in case the work-made-for-hire agreement fails for any reason
- ☑ representations and warranties
- ☑ a confidentiality provision
- ☑ a clause that addresses what happens if the work is not completed or if you stop work before it's completed
- ☑ due dates
- ☑ a clause dealing with information you give to the independent contractor to create the work and all work product, which should remain your property
- ☑ signature lines for all parties

When Someone Violates Your Copyright

Chapter 5

Copyright infringement is the violation of any of the rights in the bundle of rights explained in Chapter 2 – that is, the rights of reproduction, adaptation, distribution, public performance, and public display; the rights of attribution and integrity (see Chapter 10); and the right of importation. The Digital Millennium Copyright Act (DMCA), described in Chapter 10, extended the existing Copyright Act to specifically address works on the Internet.

What Copyright Doesn't Protect

Although it is illegal for anyone to violate any of a copyright owner's rights, these rights are not unlimited in scope, and the Copyright Act establishes certain limitations on these rights.

What You Can Do with a Copy of Copyrighted Work: The owner of a particular copy of copyrighted work – a book, for instance – that was lawfully obtained may sell or otherwise dispose of that particular copy without the authority of the copyright owner. So if you buy a book, magazine, or CD, for example, you can give it away, sell it, or even throw it away without the copyright owner's consent.

> The right of owners of copies of a copyrighted work to dispose of those copies can have interesting implications for self-published authors. For instance, at Amazon.com® each product page lists the copies sold by Amazon.com®, *and* Amazon.com® offers third parties the opportunity to sell their copies of the author's work from the same page through the Amazon Marketplace Sellers Program. Copies sold by Marketplace Sellers are *in direct competition* with the copies listed by Amazon.com®, usually at a discount. This means that self-published authors who use the Amazon.com® Advantage program to distribute their books may lose sales to third parties, who often undercut the listed price. According to the Copyright Act, however, these third parties are within their rights to dispose of their copies without the copyright owner's consent. (Note that this right does *not* apply to computer software in most cases).

Reproduction Rights for Libraries and Archives: The Copyright Act expressly permits libraries and archives to reproduce and distribute copyrighted work provided that (1) the purpose of reproduction and distribution is not for direct or indirect financial gain; and (2) the collections are available to the public or, in the case of archives, to researchers other than those already affiliated with the archive. This exception to the rights granted to copyright owners relates mostly to literary works as opposed to sound, pictorial, sculptural, or audio-visual works. But the Copyright Act limits this right to "no more than one copy … of the work."

Performances and Displays in Educational Settings: Teachers and other instructors are also exempted from the performance and display restrictions in the Copyright Act. The use must be in face-to-face teaching activities for a nonprofit educational institution, or a regular part of systematic instructional activities of a governmental body or educational institution, and must be directly related and of material assistance to the teaching process and educational content. The recipients must be students, disabled people, or government employees.

Reproduction for the Blind and Those with Other Disabilities: This exemption allows reproduction and distribution of copies of copyrighted works in particular formats suited for the blind and people with other disabilities.

Ideas, Methods, Systems: Only the actual (tangible) expression of the author can be protected by copyright. The ideas, plans, methods, or systems described or embodied in a work are not protected by copyright.

Inventions: The Copyright Act does not protect an invention or an inventive design.

Blank Forms and Similar Works: In order to be copyrightable, a work must possess a baseline amount of literary, pictorial, or musical creative expression. By its very nature, a blank form is created to record and organize rather than to creatively express information. Therefore, a form does not meet the basic creativity threshold required to render it copyrightable.

Works Containing Common Property: Copyright protection does not cover works that consist entirely of information that is common property and that is not original, such as

☑ standard calendars

☑ height and weight charts

☑ tape measures and rulers

☑ schedules of sporting events

☑ lists or tables taken from public documents or other common sources

Works Containing Both Copyrightable and Noncopyrightable Elements: So what do you do when you publish a form, calendar, or schedule not entitled to copyright protection, but it also contains original text, artwork, or some other work that is copyrightable? In this case, copyright protection extends to the copyrightable elements, namely the literary or pictorial work for which copyright protection would otherwise apply, but not to the blank form or other unprotectable aspects of the work.

Names, Pen Names, Book Titles, and Slogans

The Copyright Act does not apply to names, pen names, book titles, or slogans no matter how creative or original they may be. Therefore individual book titles; names of products, services, businesses, organizations, groups, or individual performers; advertising slogans; pen names or stage names; or the mere listing of ingredients *cannot* be copyrighted. Under certain circumstances, however, brand names, trade names, slogans, phrases, group names, and names of individuals can be protected under the laws of unfair competition and can be protected and registered under trademark law.

An author can use a pen name (pseudonym) to create a literary work. Note that nicknames or other shortened forms of an author's real name are not considered to be pen names. As stated above, the pen name itself is not subject to copyright protection. If you use a pen name, take care when filling out the registration form, to avoid supplying confusing information to the Copyright Office. In space 2 of the form, you can use your real name, or your pen name (Jolly Roger, pseudonym), or you can leave it blank. Space 4, however, requires the copyright claimant's name and should not be left blank if you are registering under a pseudonym. Note: there is no legal requirement that the author be identified by his or her real name on the application form. If you register your work under a pseudonym, consult an attorney about potential issues involved in proof of ownership.

49

 Each limitation on copyright protection has precise statutory requirements. For more information about those and other limitations and requirements, see the Copyright Act.

Determining Who Sues and Who Gets Sued

Generally speaking, the legal and beneficial owners of an exclusive right of copyright – which means the author, assignee, or exclusive licensee – have the right to sue for infringement, as long as the copyright is registered with the Copyright Office before initiating a lawsuit. But the holder of a nonexclusive right, such as a nonexclusive licensee, does not have the right to initiate an infringement suit. Limited exceptions apply in certain instances as, for example, when an individual assigns his or her copyright but retains the right to receive royalties.

Now that you know who can sue, you need to know who can be sued. There are four types of infringers.

Direct Infringer	One who actually uses copyrighted material without the consent of the copyright owner.
Contributory Infringer	One who substantially participates in the direct infringement of a copyright interest.
Vicarious Infringer	One who has the right and ability to supervise the actions of a direct infringer and has a financial stake in the infringing activity.
Criminal Infringer	One who infringes a copyright willfully either for the purpose of "commercial advantage or private financial gain," or by the reproduction or distribution of $1,000 worth of copies of copyrighted work during any 180-day period. A copyright owner must establish more than reproduction and distribution. She or he must also establish willful intent. And, in the case of felony infringement, the owner must establish that a copyright exists, that it was infringed by the defendant by reproduction and distribution of the copyrighted work, and that the defendant acted willfully, and copied or distributed at least ten copies at a value of more than $2,500 within a 180-day period.

Copyright Infringement Remedies

The Copyright Act provides four remedies for copyright infringement. Statutory damages are not available, however, if the infringement began before the work was registered, unless such registration was made *within three months after the first publication of the work.*

Injunctions: An injunction is a court declaration to stop the behavior giving rise to the lawsuit. For instance, a court may order an alleged infringer to stop making copies or to stop distributing the copyrighted work. Any court can, in its discretion, grant temporary and final injunctions "on such terms as it may deem reasonable to prevent or restrain infringement of a copyright."

Impounding Infringing Copies: When an infringement case is pending, the court has the discretion to impound all copies or phonorecords claimed to have been made or used in violation of the copyright owner's exclusive rights, and all plates, molds, matrices, masters, tapes, film negatives, or other articles by means of which such copies or phonorecords may be reproduced. If the plaintiff – the one who sues – in an infringement suit wins the case, the court can order the destruction of the copies and the methods of reproduction and distribution.

Damages and Profits: A plaintiff who wins an infringement lawsuit is entitled to either statutory damages or to actual damages and any additional profits of the infringer. If the work was registered within three months of publication, then statutory damages would be available; if not, then only actual damages would be available in addition to profits. To establish the infringer's profits, the copyright owner must present proof only of the infringer's gross revenue, and the infringer must prove his or her deductible expenses and the elements of profit attributable to factors other than the copyrighted work. If statutory damages are available, the plaintiff can recover for all infringements with respect to one work, an amount from $500 to $20,000, in the court's discretion.

In the case of willful infringement, the court has discretion to increase the damage award to a maximum of $150,000. If, however, the defendant establishes innocent infringement, the court can reduce the award to a minimum of $200.

51

Statutory damages are awarded for each infringed work, not for each incidence of infringement. For example, if someone infringes the copyrighted work *When Pigs Fly* by making one hundred illegal copies, the copyright owner can recover between $200 and $150,000, not one hundred times that amount.

Costs and Attorney Fees: The court also has the discretion to award court costs and reasonable attorney fees to the prevailing party. The court considers a number of factors, namely, the losing party's frivolousness, motivation, and objective reasonableness, and the court's need to "advance considerations of compensation and deterrents."

Limitations on Actions

Criminal infringement cases must be filed within five years of the time the infringement took place, or the case is barred. Civil infringement actions must be filed within three years after the infringement occurred, or the right to sue is forfeited. These periods of time are commonly referred to as the statute of limitations because the law limits the amount of time during which you can sue.

Other Legal Issues to Consider

Chapter 6

The First Amendment states that "Congress shall make no law ... abridging the freedom of speech, or of the press." One of the core components of the First Amendment is the freedom of speech, which protects individual expression from interference or control by the government. The Supreme Court requires a substantial justification before it will permit violation of this right. But some speech that would breach the peace or might cause violence has been prohibited. Perhaps the best-known example is the prohibition against yelling "fire" in a crowded theater.

Some scholars and critics suggest that the First Amendment conflicts with an author's right under the Copyright Act (based on Article I, Section 8 of the Constitution) to hold exclusive rights to his or her creations. At least in theory, however, both sections of the Constitution work together to balance the rights of the individual with the rights of society as a whole. For example the First Amendment allows the free exchange of ideas while the Copyright Act protects the individual's physical manifestation of those ideas.

Still, this balance tips in favor of free speech and society, and against copyright protection, when copyrighted material is so newsworthy that courts may declare it is in the public interest to share certain work without the copyright owner's permission. For instance, in the federal district court case of *Time Inc. v. Bernard Geis Assoc.*, the court permitted public use of copyrighted film footage of the assassination of President John F. Kennedy without the copyright owner's consent.

Using Someone's Name or Likeness in Your Work

Cashing in on one's celebrity is big business these days. Salaries for sports and entertainment figures are certainly impressive. But these million-dollar salaries are often dwarfed when compared to the multimillion-dollar deals based on using a person's name or image to endorse a product or service.

This use of a person's name or likeness for commercial gain involves one of the lesser known intellectual property rights – the right of publicity. The right of publicity is a person's exclusive right to use, and to prevent the unauthorized use of, his or her name, likeness, or other aspect of his or her persona (collectively referred to as persona) for commercial gain. The definition of "persona" goes beyond a person's image and can include words or sounds that are intended to remind the audience of the person, a look-alike, a nickname or phrase commonly associated with the person, and even his or her former name. Therefore, the potential for a right-of-publicity claim exists any time you use someone's persona (or an imitation of it) in your book, article, or other literary or artistic work.

The first case to acknowledge the right of publicity was *Haelan Laboratories Inc. v. Topps Chewing Gum, Inc.* in 1953, in which the court recognized the valuable property right of a baseball player's photograph when used on trading cards. In a prominent right-of-publicity case, *White v. Samsung Electronics America, Inc.* (1993), the court found that an advertisement which featured a set similar to the *Wheel of Fortune* show and a robotic Vanna White look-alike infringed Vanna White's right of publicity. The court found in her favor and extended the right-of-publicity protection to include not only name and likeness but also identity.

In September 2002, Tom Cruise and Nicole Kidman sued Sephora, Inc., a cosmetics company, in a Los Angeles court for allegedly using a picture of them without permission in a brochure to advertise the company's so-called celebrity scents. They sued under several legal theories, including California's common law right of publicity and unfair competition, and under the Lanham Act.

There is no federally protected right of publicity. This right is protected by common law developed by cases in some states and by state statute developed by legislative bodies in others. In fact, some states refer to this right as the right of publicity but others do not; instead, they protect the right under other legal theories such as the right of privacy or unfair competition (defined as appropriating the commercial value of a person's identity by using the person's name, likeness, or other characteristics of identity without consent for purposes of trade).

Also, while most states protect the rights of both celebrities and noncelebrities, a minority of states protect the right of publicity for celebrities only. The rationale for only protecting celebrities seems to be based on the argument that a noncelebrity's persona has no commercial value. There are some general guidelines and exceptions, however, that have emerged from this

54

piecemeal set of state laws dealing with the right of publicity. In some cases a public figure's heirs have a legal right of publicity in the dead person's name, voice, signature, photograph, or likeness (for example, under California Civil Code 3344.1).

The absence of a federal right-of-publicity law and the wide differences in laws from state to state becomes more and more problematic as technology continues to increase exponentially the ways in which publicity rights can be violated either innocently or with intent. There is talk of a federal law; however, although desperately needed, none exists yet.

Exceptions: The two main exceptions to the right of publicity, the newsworthiness exception and the incidental use exception, are based on the First Amendment's balance between free speech and the right of publicity.

The newsworthiness exception allows a person's name or likeness to be used in a news story without that person's consent as long as the use is considered to be of legitimate public interest or concern. Furthermore, the use cannot mislead the reader into thinking that the person endorses the article, newspaper, book, or whatever vehicle his or her persona appears in. A common way that writers can protect themselves when writing about others is to include a disclaimer making it clear that those others do not endorse the writing.

The exception for incidental use occurs when a person's name is merely mentioned or his or her likeness is used or referred to. If this exception did not exist, the right of publicity could very well stifle creativity. For instance, authors would not be able to authenticate a story line by referring to real people and places. The use should be reasonably related to the content of your article, book, or other literary work. The test is whether the use is of interest or concern to the public. This test extends not only to hard news stories but also to sports, entertainment, and similar pieces.

Uses of Someone's Persona: As discussed above, an individual's persona can be used to advertise a product or service. Such use is considered a commercial use. Commercial speech has been defined as doing no more than proposing a commercial transaction (see *Hoffman v. Capital Cities*, 2001). Although commercial speech is entitled to some measure of protection under the First Amendment, it is limited. And where the sole purpose of the use is to sell a product or service, no First Amendment protection exists.

55

Note, however, that it may be permissible to use an individual's persona to help sell a product or service if the use is reasonably related to the content. For instance, *Hoffman v. Capital Cities* resulted because *Los Angeles Magazine* used a photograph of Dustin Hoffman's character image Tootsie as an illustration for the article "Grand Illusions" in the "Fabulous Hollywood" issue. Sixteen other stills from familiar movie scenes were also used in the article that discussed 1997 spring fashions. The caption under the picture in question read, "Dustin Hoffman isn't a drag in a butter-colored silk gown by Richard Tyler and Ralph Lauren heels." The magazine did not obtain permission from Hoffman (the subject) or from the copyright owner (who is generally the photographer who took the picture).

The court found that the use was not pure commercial speech because the picture did not appear in a Ralph Lauren ad or a Richard Tyler ad. Furthermore, in terms of the context of the article, the court found that the use combines fashion photography, humor, and editorial comment on classic films and famous actors.

Use of someone's persona may also be permissible if editorial in nature, that is, if used for news reporting; scholarship; or cultural, historical, educational, political, and public interest reasons. The same consideration is given to artistic use in which an individual's name or likeness appears in a work of fiction that incorporates real people. Again, this use is probably permissible as long as the goal is artistic and of public interest and concern rather than for purely economic gain.

Who Is Entitled to Sue to Protect the Right of Publicity: Most states require a right-of-publicity claimant to be a living person. But a few jurisdictions, most notably California, allow heirs of a deceased person to sue. For the law in your state, contact an attorney familiar with intellectual property and privacy laws in your area.

Defending a Right-of-Publicity Claim: Schuyler M. Moore, Esq., explains in his article "Raising Defenses to Right-of-Publicity Claims" that there is no consistent set of defenses to such claims. The absence of clearly defined laws and defenses presents a major issue for writers who expose themselves to potential right-of-publicity claims with the mere mention of another person's name or likeness in a literary work.

Furthermore, even if you successfully defend your use of a person's name or likeness in your manuscript, you still lose by being sued in the first place and having to defend a costly lawsuit. Publishing houses hesitate to expose themselves to such liability; to anticipate and avoid it, they subject manuscripts to legal vetting, which means they review manuscripts thoroughly for legal issues. Self-published authors are certainly not immune from legal liability and should submit their manuscripts to the same vetting process. With the potential for professional and personal liability, a self-published author is at greater risk than a large publishing house, which employs an entire legal department devoted exclusively to these issues. Therefore, if you decide to publish your work independently, you should submit your manuscript to a publishing attorney who can vet it, alert you to possible legal issues, and advise you on the best course of action.

Privacy Issues

The American Heritage Dictionary defines the right of privacy as "the quality or condition of being secluded from the presence or view of others." More simply put, it is the right to be left alone. The three generally recognized invasions of privacy include intrusion, unreasonable publicity, and false light.

Intrusion occurs when someone intentionally enters without permission into a place where you have a reasonable expectation of privacy. Intrusion involves issues such as hidden cameras or other surveillance methods, wire tapping, and searching someone's garbage. Therefore, when conducting interviews, you should always inform the subject that you are taping the conversation. To further protect yourself, you should require all interviewees to sign a permission form 📰 authorizing you to tape the conversation and use the content in your literary work. In the case of intrusion claims, a plaintiff is not required to show that the alleged intruder divulged the information obtained to the public. It is sufficient to show that the person entered a place where the plaintiff had a reasonable expectation of privacy (his or her home, for instance).

Unreasonable publicity occurs when intimate or embarrassing facts about a person are divulged to the public (published) in an unfair or irrational way. A court finds such publication to be unreasonable when the information is not of public interest or concern. And it is not enough to argue that the information is true. In fact, privacy laws are intended to protect against the publication of truthful but private information.

False light occurs when a person is portrayed in public in an extremely offensive way. The classic example is when an offensive caption appears beneath someone's picture, a caption that could leave a false and negative impression of the individual in the mind of a reasonable person. A false-light claim can also arise when essential facts are omitted; as for example when a reporter writes that a man was arrested for molesting his seven-year-old son but fails to report that all charges were subsequently dropped when it was discovered the father was out of town during the incident; or when certain elements of a book are fictionalized but it is not clear what is fact and what is fiction, a situation that can be avoided with a clear, well-written disclaimer.

When It Is OK to Discuss Intimate Facts: Authors are generally permitted to discuss facts that are generally known to the public or are considered newsworthy. But here's a general list of materials that are considered off limits: private letters, e-mail messages, information about sexual proclivities or sexual history, financial or medical information, or other private matters. When discussing the lives of noncelebrities, remember that it is even more difficult to establish that the information is of public concern or interest. The sex life of Madonna, Bill Clinton, or Earvin "Magic" Johnson may be worthy of a tell-all unauthorized biography, but that may not be true of your ex-spouse, unless he or she also happens to be a public figure whose affairs would be considered of public concern or interest.

E-Mail and Privacy

As part of the technology boom of the '80s and '90s, millions of Americans now use e-mail as a quick and inexpensive way to communicate with friends, family, and colleagues both near and far. People assume that e-mail is also secure; however e-mail is far less secure than traditional mail. E-mail, like other types of electronic communication, such as cell phones and pagers, is susceptible to illegal interception. Under the Electronic Communications Privacy Act of 1986 (ECPA), third parties are prohibited from reading private e-mail.

The ECPA extended privacy law to cover new technologies like e-mail, so you must take care to obtain the necessary permissions if you intend to incorporate e-mail messages into your manuscript. Also recognize that e-mail is not a 100-percent-secure communication environment. A good rule of thumb is not to e-mail anything that you would not want sent instantly to millions of people. With one click of the mouse, the recipient could do just that.

Trademark
Chapter 7

Like other business people, Literary Entrepreneurs use trademarks or brands on their products and services to identify them and distinguish them from those of their competitors. The terms *trademark, brand,* and *brand name* are often used interchangeably. A trademark identifies the source of a product or service (which company or individual produces or distributes it), and a brand or brand name is the name given to a certain product or service. Many brands, however, may not be suitable for federal trademark registration yet may clearly identify a certain person, product, or service. For example, Yellow Pages, if used for the business pages of a telephone book, is not suitable for federal trademark because it is generic; yet, it is a very strong brand. But The Real Yellow Pages®, The Friendly Yellow Pages®, The Original Yellow Pages®, and 1-800-Yellow Pages® are among the many registered trademarks using the term (brand) Yellow Pages.

Contrary to popular belief, trademarks come into existence the moment you use them to mark your goods or services for your customers. That is worth repeating: trademarks come into existence the moment you use them to mark your goods or services for your customers. You do not have to register your trademark with any governmental agency to bring your trademark into existence. In fact you cannot register your trademark until you have used it with your goods or services. The longer you use your mark, the stronger it becomes — because it builds goodwill and recognition with your customers. This unregistered use of a trademark is protected under common law.

Trademarks registered under federal and state laws as well as certain unregistered trademarks under common law enjoy exclusive rights. A federally registered trademark will generally give you the right to use the mark in all fifty states and all U.S. territories. A federal trademark also protects consumers by preventing different businesses in the United States from using the same or similar trademarks, which helps to avoid confusion among products and their sources. Protection of trademarks registered under state law is limited to the state of registration; the rules and regulations that affect trademarks vary from state to state. Trademark protections of common law are limited to the geographic area in which the mark has actually been used. The fact that many trademarked products are now marketed and sold via the World Wide Web to a large interstate audience means that a broad common law protection may cover them.

? Is there such a thing as an international trademark?

Answer: No. Although trademarks are available in most foreign countries, registration must be applied for in each of those countries. Under certain international treaties and agreements, including the Madrid Protocol and the Community Trademark in Europe, filing may be made in multiple countries. The president signed the Madrid Protocol trademark treaty into law on November 2, 2002. This will allow U.S. trademark owners to file for registration in any member country by filing a single standardized application in English, with a single set of fees, through the USPTO.

Trademark and Service Mark Defined

A trademark or service mark is one way to identify certain goods or services as those produced or provided by a specific person or company. A service mark is the same as a trademark except that it applies to the source of a service rather than a product. The terms *trademark, mark,* and *brand* are often used interchangeably to refer to both trademarks and service marks, whether they consist of word marks or other types of marks, which will be described below. They may be names, slogans, logos, designs, or other identifying marks. Trademarks date back to about 4000 B.C., when different markings were used to identify property belonging to specific owners. Craftsmen reproduced their marks or brands on their products. Farmers branded their livestock, and royal families identified their ancestry with a specific coat of arms.

Over the years this identification method evolved into today's system of trademark registration and protection. This system helps consumers identify and purchase a product or service that meets their needs because its unique trademark indicates its nature and quality. United States law defines "trademark" as a word, phrase, symbol, or design, or a combination of words, phrases, symbols, or designs that identifies and distinguishes the source of the goods or services of one party from those of others.

If in the application for federal registration you enter all the words of your mark in capital letters and in a standard font, then the registered word or term may be used in any way (upper case, lower case, on its side, in various colors, in squiggly lines, and so forth), and the protection still exists. If the words are entered on the application in upper and lower case, then the registered mark is considered a drawing, and you are protected only for the specific way in which it appears on the application.

Trademarks may consist of:

☑ Word mark – one word or a group of words (AMISTAD®, DEF POETRY JAM™)

☑ Drawing mark – a black-and-white drawing of words, letters, and/or numbers in stylized form ᴮᴸᴬᶜᴷ*expressions*

☑ Persona – the name or persona of a real person (George Foreman Grills; Oprah's Book Club®)

☑ Symbol mark – logo or design (the Golden Arches of McDonald's; the Nike swoosh)

☑ Three-dimensional mark – the shape and packaging of goods (Coca Cola bottles; yellow-and-black boxes for Kodak Film)

☑ Sound mark – musical, vocal, electronic, or other sound (NBC chimes; AAMCO honk)

☑ Fragrance mark – (smell of plumeria blossoms on embroidery yarn)

☑ Color mark – color schemes or a single color used as a distinguishing feature (pink fiberglass insulation of Corning; colorful plumage of the NBC Peacock)

Normally, a mark for goods appears on the product or on its packaging, label, instruction manual, and container; a service mark appears in advertising and other printed matter related to the services, such as announcements, brochures, publicity releases, invoices, stationery, and business cards. Trademarks indicate to consumers that a particular product comes from a certain source, even if the name of that source is unknown to the consumer. For example, when you go to the grocery store you buy CHIQUITA® bananas. The source of the bananas is unknown to you, but you know that CHIQUITA® brand bananas are consistently tasty and of high quality. Trademarks also create goodwill for their owners by exploiting the established quality and reputation built up over time.

61

Some examples of registered trademarks and service marks are:

☑ **Essence®** (goods and services) *Owner:* Essence Communications, Inc. For magazine and entertainment services.

☑ **Black Expressions®** ᴮᴸᴬᶜᴷ*expressions* (goods and services) *Owner:* Doubleday Direct, Inc. Mail order book clubs; online retail store services featuring books, prerecorded audio cassettes of music and books readings, prerecorded video cassettes, and gift merchandise.

☑ **Oprah's Book Club®** (services) for Oprah's TV and online book club. *Owner:* Harpo, Inc. Entertainment services rendered via television; namely, a series of programs involving book discussion groups, and meetings and discussions with authors, and relating to books, authors, and reading; and online services provided by means of a global computer information network featuring interactive discussion groups with authors, readers, and book lovers, and relating to books, authors, and reading.

☑ **Harry Potter®** **Harry Potter** (goods) *Owner:* TIME WARNER ENTERTAINMENT COMPANY, L.P., American Television and Communications Corporation, and Warner Communications Inc. Books, paper items, ceramics, lithographs; pens, pencils, and cases for them; erasers, crayons, markers, colored pencils, painting sets, chalk and chalkboards; decals, games, action figures, clothing.

☑ **FUBU®** ***FUBU*** (goods) *Owner:* GTFM, Inc. Clothing, namely shirts, vests, sweaters, shoes, caps, bandannas, shorts, sweatshirts, pants, belts for clothing, socks, swimwear, jackets, rainwear, blouses, dresses, footwear, hosiery, scarves, hats, headbands, pajamas, and sleepwear.

☑ **Strivers Row®** (goods) *Owner:* Random House, Inc. House mark for a series of fiction and nonfiction books on a variety of topics.

Choosing a Trademark

The trademark you choose is important and may be critical to the success of your business. You must answer three important questions when deciding on a trademark: first, does the trademark adequately reflect your image; second, is it available; and third, how strong is it.

Finding a Trademark That Adequately Reflects Your Image

Defining the image you want to project through your trademark is a business decision that should reflect a strategy which may follow you and your business through your lifetime and beyond. It is important for you to think about your trademark in light of the type of goods and services that you will provide, your existing trademarks, and those of your competitors. Consider these questions: Do you intend to build a series around your book or publication? Is it your persona that will drive all of your business endeavors? Have you created a captivating character in your writing? Do you want to establish a new genre that will be defined by your work? Do you want to establish your business as *the* source of expertise in a narrow area?

Seek professional help in crafting your trademark or brand as you answer these and other questions. The right trademark or brand for yourself, your business, or your work can bring great economic rewards.

Trademark Availability

A search of registered and unregistered marks, preferably by an attorney or a well-qualified search group, should be performed to find out whether the trademark you want – a word, name, logo, slogan, sound, color, design, fragrance, or some combination of those – is available. Searches can be performed at the United States Patent and Trademark Office (USPTO or PTO) Web site (http://tess.uspto.gov); however, those searches only cover trademark applications that have been filed in the PTO. It is important to search not only your proposed trademark but also variations of it. Also, for companies that market or intend to market their goods and services in an international market, international (and foreign word) searches are a must.

The PTO Public Search Library for trademarks, located at 2900 Crystal Drive, 2nd Floor, Arlington, Virginia 22202, is open between 8:00 A.M. and 5:30 P.M., and use is free to the public. Also, certain information may be searched at a Patent and Trademark Depository Library. These libraries have CD-ROMs containing the database of registered and pending marks, but they do not show images of the design marks.

More comprehensive searches may include state registries, domain names, telephone directories, databases, and periodicals. A number of commercial Internet sites provide these services. Be cautious, though; thoroughly investigate anyone you do business with on the Internet.

Preliminary Internet searches for words may be conducted using search engines, such as Google, Lycos, Excite, and Yahoo! Domain names may be searched at www.networksolutions.com or a number of other commercial Internet sites, some free and some for a fee. The more time, money, and effort you devote to promoting your trademarked goods or services, the greater your need to search the mark thoroughly.

If you use a mark that is registered to another individual or company, that use may result in a lawsuit, with penalties ranging from stopping your use of the trademark to monetary fines. It is always better to do an extensive preliminary review and search before investing a great deal of money and other resources in marketing a trademark that may not be available or suitable for registration.

63

The Strength of Uniqueness

You should choose a distinctive trademark – one that is different from all known marks. Novelty carries strength. For instance Xerox® is a distinctive trademark that had no meaning or definition until the owner created it. You can create a new word too. There are several levels of distinctiveness, ranging from fanciful (the word has no previous meaning, such as KODAK®) to arbitrary (a word that has meaning but is not associated with the goods or services offered, such as IVORY® when used with soap) to suggestive (the word has some descriptive aspect but requires some imagination to identify it with your goods and services, such as BEAUTYREST® when used with mattresses).

Federal trademark registration is not available for marks that merely describe an ingredient, quality, characteristic, function, feature, purpose, or use of the relevant goods or services. An exception exists for descriptive marks that have been in existence for a long time and have developed recognition.

> *Oprah's Book Club*® is a distinctive and strong mark. Oprah has a unique name. Customers (viewers) immediately associate the service with the provider of the service. *Best Seller Book Club* describes the service it offers. It is a book club offering best-seller books to its customers. Thus, it is a weak mark that is not suitable for federal trademark protection. But if the *Best Seller Book Club* has been in existence for five or more years and is well known in the literary community, federal registration is possible if the mark has developed a strong secondary meaning over time.

A generic mark, the actual name of a good or service, is not registrable. For example, you cannot trademark the word "book" for a book, "audio book club" for a book club featuring electronically recorded books, or "computer" for a computer. Apple® is a strong arbitrary trademark for a computer, however, because it has a meaning that has nothing to do with the product.

If a registered trademark becomes the general name for a product, over time it will lose its registered trademark status. For example, kleenex, aspirin, and band-aid were once registered trademarks that have lost their distinctiveness because they have become general product names. Any company can use these names to describe its products. But all is not necessarily lost. Owners of generic marks can use novel designs or slogans to get federal registered trademark protection, within the context of the new design or slogan, for marks that have otherwise lost their registration.

Registered marks that became generic and were reclaimed through novel designs or slogans include **Kleenex**

To protect a trademark from becoming generic, a careful strategy must be used. Often trademark holders will monitor their marks to prevent their misuse. For instance, vendors are careful to serve only Coca Cola® when Coca Cola® is asked for and not any other cola product because the owner of the Coca-Cola® trademark is vigilant in maintaining it and strategically watches proprietors who sell its product. The trademark owner wants to make sure that the mark is not diluted by being used to identify any and every cola product rather than Coca Cola® exclusively.

Federal Trademark Registration

Federal registration is not required to establish rights in a trademark. Common law rights arise from actual use of a mark. Generally, the first individual or entity to either use a mark in commerce or file an Intent to Use application with the Patent and Trademark Office has the ultimate right to use and to register the mark. Also, if a trademark owner stops using a trademark, the registration ceases to exist.

Federal trademark registration has many advantages, however. It allows for

☑ constructive notice nationwide of the trademark owner's claim

☑ evidence of ownership of the trademark

☑ invoking the jurisdiction of federal courts

☑ use as a basis for obtaining registration in a foreign country

☑ filing with the U.S. Customs Service to prevent importation of infringing foreign goods

65

Trademark Issues Specific to Authors

A Single Creative Work versus a Series: Usually, the title of just one creative work – one book, one record or compact disc, one video, one play – may not be trademarked because the title describes the contents of that one creative work itself and does not lead you to its source or identify its source. For example, *Black Coffee, Grand Daddy's Dirt*, and *Married But Still Looking* are all titles of single books. Also, the name of a character in a single book is not usually thought to function as a trademark even if it forms part of the title, as Little Lulu does in *Little Lulu Goes To Market*.

When a book title acts as a single identifying source for a series, however, it then serves as a trademark for the series. Examples include *Chicken Soup for the Soul®* and *Harry Potter®*.

Pen Names: A pen name, or pseudonym, is a name a writer uses that is different from his or her legal name. Pen names, even if used in a series, do not function as trademarks.

Characters: A character from a series of books, even when used repeatedly in that series, is usually not given trademark registration. But trademark protection may be given depending on how the character is used in connection with goods. Only when the character is an identifying source for the author or the series can that character serve as a trademark. Examples include Mickey Mouse®, Nancy Drew®, and Little Bill®. Each immediately identifies its source of goods.

Articles, Columns, and Features in Publications: Portions or sections of publications, such as chapters or subsections of books or columns and features of newspapers or magazines, are not usually considered separate goods but are part of the publication. People usually buy the publication – the magazine, newspaper, or book – based on the mark that identifies it and not the feature or section title as the source of the information.

For example if you read an article titled "Self-Published Authors" in *Black Issues Book Review Magazine (BIBR)*, you are more likely to remember that you read the article in *BIBR* than to remember the name of the author.

Name of Recording Artist or Group on One Recording: Similarly, the name of a recording artist or group on one recording is not registrable as a trademark for that recording. If the artist or group's name has appeared on a series of recordings, however, the artist's name or designation identifies the source and is registrable as a trademark.

> The author and performance poet L.I.F.E.® has trademarked his name, as have OPRAH® and IYANLA®. When your name clearly identifies the source of services and goods that you provide, it is suitable for trademark protection. A trademark is a valuable property asset of the artist or author.

Online Publications: Internet publications such as e-newsletters, e-bulletins, and e-zines are a popular phenomenon. These online publications are considered a service rather than a product and are registrable under existing trademark laws.

The Anatomy of a Trademark Application

Chapter 8

You may apply for federal trademark registration in two ways:

☞ If you are already using a mark in interstate commerce – selling goods or services in two or more states – you may file an application based on that use.

☞ If you have not yet used the mark, you may file an intent-to-use application based on a bona fide intention to use it in interstate commerce. The United States Patent and Trademark Office (USPTO or PTO) will approve the mark based on that filing. But to register it, you must file an allegation of use within six months of receiving that approval. If necessary, you may file for an extension.

For the purpose of obtaining federal registration, *commerce* means all business or financial transactions that may lawfully be regulated by the U.S. Congress, such as commerce between states or between the United States and another country. Of course in the twenty-first century most companies will conduct business using the Internet and will reach potential customers throughout the world, thereby meeting the use-in-commerce requirement.

What makes use bona fide?

Bona fide means in good faith. Use of a mark in the ordinary course of trade, with no intent to deceive, and not only to reserve a right in a mark, is bona fide. For instance, if you live in California, selling one or two books to your cousin in Maryland may not be enough to show a bona fide use in interstate commerce if this is an advance order that you cannot ship to her yet. But if you are in the business of selling books over the Internet or through direct mail, and you sell and ship two books to your cousin in Maryland from your office in California, that would be bona fide use.

67

Things to Consider before Federal Registration of Your Trademark

☞ Use of a trademark in promotion or advertising before the product or service is actually available for sale to the general public does not qualify as use in commerce.

☞ Use of a mark in local commerce within a state (intrastate commerce) does not qualify as use in commerce. But states do offer trademark protection for intrastate commerce.

Once you have determined which is the most appropriate form for you – In Use or Intent to Use – you can prepare the trademark application.

Preparing the Trademark Application

The PTO has declared that it intends to become a paperless office and has taken giant steps in that direction. In keeping with that goal, the PTO prefers that you file your application for registration of a trademark over the Internet, using the Trademark Electronic Application System (TEAS) discussed below and available at http://www.uspto.gov or on the PTO's preprinted scannable form. You may also obtain the PTO form by calling the Trademark Assistance Center at 703-308-9000 or 800-786-9199. Nonetheless, it is still good practice to keep a paper copy and transmission receipt of everything you send to the PTO, whether via snail mail or over the Internet.

The PTO strongly discourages self-created forms but will accept them if they meet the basic requirements for receipt of a filing date. (The filing date is the official indication that the PTO has not only received but has accepted your application as filed and that the review process has begun.) If you do use a self-created form, it should be on letter-size paper (8½ by 11 inches), type-written, double spaced, with margins of at least 1½ inches at the left and top. The application should be written on only one side of the paper.

The Applicant: A registration application must be filed by the mark's owner or, in the case of an intent-to-use application, by the person who is entitled to use the mark in commerce. Normally owners are the people who apply the mark to goods they produce, or use the mark in the sale or advertising of services they perform.

68

Applicants may be individuals or juristic persons. Juristic persons include corporations, partnerships, joint ventures, unions, associations, and other organizations capable of suing and being sued in a court of law. An operating division, or the like, which is merely an organizational unit of a company and not a legal entity that can sue and be sued, may not own or apply to register a mark.

Verification: You must verify your trademark application by submitting either a signed oath or a declaration to attest to the truth of the important parts of the application and knowledge of the penalties for false statements.

A signed verification is not required for receipt of an application filing date. If the initial application does not include a proper verified statement, the PTO will require you to submit a verified statement that relates back to the original filing date.

Identifying and Classifying Goods and Services: You must include in your trademark application a list of the particular goods or services on or in connection with which you use or intend to use your mark. You should designate the appropriate international class number(s) for the identified goods or services, if you know this information. Classification information is available on the PTO Web site at www.uspto.gov/trademark. It is a good practice to search registered trademarks used for similar goods or services to see what classifications they may have used.

The Basis for Filing: Before a mark will be approved for registration, an application must specify and meet the requirements of one or more of these four filing bases:

☑ use of a mark in interstate commerce

☑ bona fide intention to use a mark in interstate commerce

☑ a claim of priority, based on a foreign application filed earlier

☑ registration of a mark in the applicant's country of origin

Submission of Drawings: You must submit a drawing of your trademark with your original application in order to receive a filing date, except in applications for registration of sound, scent, and other nonvisual marks. The drawing is used to reproduce the mark in the *Official Gazette* and on the registration certificate.

The main purpose of the drawing is to provide notice of the nature of the mark to be registered. The drawing is promptly entered into the automated records of the PTO and is available to the public through Trademark Electronic Search System (TESS) on the PTO Web site at http://tess.uspto.gov. You may submit drawings in one of two forms: special-form drawings or typed drawings.

Typed Drawings: The drawing may be typed if the mark consists only of words, letters, numbers, common forms of punctuation, or any combination of these elements. In a typed drawing, every word or letter must be typed in capital letters. Typed drawings give you a broader trademark because your application does not limit the mark to any special form or lettering. The mark in your drawing must agree with the mark as used on the specimens in your application.

Special-Form Drawings: Stylized or special-form drawings, also referred to as ink drawings, present marks that contain special characteristics, such as elements of design or color, styles of lettering, or unusual forms of punctuation. All special-form drawings must be of a quality that will reproduce satisfactorily on a black-and-white photocopier. Only black and white may appear on the drawing. If your mark includes color, it must be represented by particular patterns and shadings of gray. If the drawing is not of a quality that will reproduce satisfactorily for scanning into the PTO's database, and for printing in the *Official Gazette* and on the certificate of registration, the PTO will require a new drawing.

Specimens: You must submit a specimen, a sample that shows the mark as actually used on the goods or with the services. The specimen for a trademark for goods is a duplicate of the goods, a label or tag, commercial packaging, or a display associated with the goods bearing the trademark. If the nature of the goods makes it impractical for you to place the mark on any of those things, then documents associated with the goods or their sale may be used. Advertising, brochures, fact sheets, and telephone directories that show use of your trademark are not acceptable specimens for goods.

A specimen for your service mark application is use of your mark in the sale or advertising of your services. Service mark specimens may include newspaper, magazine, and radio advertisements; brochures, billboards, handbills, and direct mail leaflets; and representations of computer screens. Invoices may be acceptable service mark specimens provided they show your mark and refer to the relevant services. Letterhead, stationery, or business cards having your mark are acceptable if and only if the services are clearly shown either within the mark itself or somewhere on the paper.

Filing Costs: Your trademark application must include a filing fee for each class of goods or services that you submit, and the fee must be received before your application can be given a filing date. You may pay by credit card, check, money order, or through an existing PTO deposit account. The fee schedule is listed at http://www.uspto.gov/main/howtofees.htm. The fees change annually; as of this writing the filing fee is $325.00 per class.

Where to File: The application and all other correspondence should be addressed to the Assistant Commissioner for Trademarks, 2900 Crystal Drive, Arlington, Virginia 22202-3513. The initial application should be directed to Box NEW APP FEE. An Amendment to Allege Use should be directed to Attn. AAU. A Statement of Use or request for an extension should be directed to Box ITU FEE. Trademark applications may not be filed by fax.

PTO Serial Numbers: Each trademark application received by the PTO receives a serial number that identifies it. Once the PTO assigns a serial number, you should refer to that number in all written and telephone communications about your application. The serial number is generally an eight-digit number, such as 78/123456.

Enclosing a Postcard: When you submit a trademark application by mail it is advisable to include a stamped, self-addressed postcard with it. The postcard should specifically list each item in the mailing, namely, the written application, the drawing, the fee, and the specimens (if appropriate). The PTO will stamp the filing date and serial number of the application on the postcard to acknowledge receipt. These will help you if any item is later lost or if you wish to inquire about your application. The PTO will send a separate official notification of the filing date and serial number for every application about two months after receipt.

Filing with TEAS – the Trademark Electronic Application System

The PTO has streamlined the trademark application process with TEAS, which allows you to fill out an application form and check it for completeness over the Internet. The TEAS system is divided into two parts, e-TEAS and PrinTEAS. Using e-TEAS, you can submit the application directly to the PTO online, paying by credit card, e-check, or through an existing PTO deposit account. Using PrinTEAS, you can fill in the application on the screen, print it out, and mail it to the PTO along with payment. It's your choice. Both e-TEAS and PrinTEAS are available from http://teas.uspto.gov/indexTLT.html.

71

Correct Use of the Symbols ™, ᔆᴹ, and ®

Anyone who claims rights in a mark may use the superscript ™ (trademark) or ᔆᴹ (service mark) designation with the mark to alert the public to the claim. It is not necessary to register or even have a pending application to use these designations. Of course your claim may or may not be valid.

The registration symbol, ®, may be used only when your mark is registered in the PTO. It is improper and illegal to use this symbol at any time before the registration has been issued. Be sure to omit all symbols from the mark in the drawing you submit with your application; the symbols are not considered part of the mark. If you cannot find the ™ or ™ symbols on your computer, change the font to superscript (under Format>Font in Microsoft Word) and type ™ or ™.

Maintaining Trademark Registration

Rights in a federally registered trademark have an initial term of ten years. Federal registrations, however, can last indefinitely if the owner

☑ continues to use the mark on or in connection with the goods and/or services in the registration

☑ files all the necessary documentation in the PTO at the right time

☑ pays the requisite fees at the appropriate times

The owner of a registered mark must periodically file

☑ Affidavits of Continued Use or Excusable Nonuse, with applicable fee

☑ Applications of Renewal, with applicable fee

Forms for filing these documents are available at http://www.uspto.gov. PTO fees are adjusted annually.

Cancellation of Trademark

The PTO will not send you a notice or a reminder. To avoid cancellation of your trademark registrations, remember to put the important renewal dates in your calendar and file all required documents and fees on time.

Filing for Continued Use: Six years from the date of your registration you must file a Declaration of Use (Section 8 Declaration), stating that you still use the mark, and you must submit specimens showing how the mark is being used. Your Declaration of Use may be filed as early as year five. The PTO provides a six-month grace period after the six-year deadline to allow you to file a late declaration, for an additional late filing fee. If you fail to file a Declaration of Use on time, you can lose your registration and be forced to file a new application.

Renewing: A renewal application, along with another Declaration of Continued Use and accompanying specimens, must be filed between the ninth and tenth year from the date of your registration. The PTO provides a six-month grace period after the ten-year deadline to allow you to file a late renewal and declaration. Renewal fees may be paid as early as year nine from the date of registration. Trademark registrations may be renewed every ten years thereafter for as long as you continue to use your mark in connection with your goods or services. 📋

Registering a Trademark in a Foreign Country

Almost all countries register and protect trademarks. Each national or regional office maintains a register of trademarks that contains full application information on all registrations and renewals, and facilitates examination, search, and potential opposition by third parties. The effects of regional or national registration are, however, limited to the country or region concerned.

The United States is a member of the Paris Convention, which is a treaty between 140 member countries relating to trademarks and other intellectual property. Each member country guarantees to the citizens of the other countries the same rights in trademark matters that it gives to its own citizens. The treaty also allows that, on the basis of an application filed in one of the member countries, you may, within a certain period of time, apply for protection in all the other member countries.

To avoid the need to register separately with each national or regional office, the World Intellectual Property Organization (WIPO) administers a system of international registration of marks. Two treaties govern the WIPO system: the Madrid Agreement Concerning the International Registration of Marks and the Madrid Protocol. A person who has a relationship (through nationality, domicile, or business address) with a member country of the Madrid Agreement or the Madrid Protocol, on the basis of a registration or application with the trademark office of that country, may obtain an international registration having effect in some or all of the other countries in the Madrid Union.

At present more than seventy countries are party to one or both of the agreements. For a list of member nations, see www.wipo.org/madrid/en/index. html. On November 2, 2002, the president signed into law an authorization act, H.R. 2215, which implements the accession of the United States to the Madrid Protocol trademark treaty. As of November 2, 2003, U.S. trademark owners will be able to register for trademark protection in any member country by filing a single application in the USPTO. 📋

73

Trademarks on the Internet
Chapter 9

The Internet is the single most important tool (outside of your creative genius) that you need as a Literary Entrepreneur in the year 2003 and beyond. Whether you use it for research, marketing, e-mail discussion groups related to your literary interests, or filing your trademark application online, the Internet is essential. And most likely you'll want to have your own Web site to display and market your literary efforts. Therefore you need to know something about domain names and trademarks online.

Domain Names

A domain name, sometimes called a URL (uniform resource locator), identifies the address of a particular Web site. Your domain name may be any unique combination of letters and numerals that suits your fancy, as long as it doesn't already belong to someone else.

Domain names are divided into two or more parts separated by a period that we refer to as a dot. The part of a domain name that precedes the last dot is called the second-level domain name; the part after the last dot is called the extension or top-level domain name. For example, in www.fyos.com, the top level is com, and the second level is fyos.

Top-Level Domain Names

Top-level domain names (TLDs) are the highest category and include two types: generic (gTLD) and country coded (ccTLD). No doubt you are familiar with the gTLDs that have been in use for years: .com (commercial), .org (organizational), .edu (educational), .gov (governmental), and .net (network).

On November 16, 2000, ICANN (Internet Corporation for Assigned Names and Numbers) selected seven new gTLDs, which can be registered only through ICANN-accredited registrars and their resellers. You can find a list of accredited registrars on the InterNIC site at www.internic.net/regist.html. The new domain identifiers include .aero (airlines), .biz (general business), .coop (registered cooperative societies), .info (general use), .museum (accredited museums), .name (personal names, e-mail, and Web sites), and .pro (for professionals, including doctors, lawyers, and accountants). The .pro registry is not operational or accepting domains yet; for further information contact http://www.nic.pro. Three of these new gTLDs – .aero, .museum, and .coop – are sponsored, meaning that they are operated by specific interest groups which have established limiting criteria for use of the extensions.

At present, 192 countries have their own registry authorities, each with its own operating regulations. Two examples of such ccTLDS are .vg (British Virgin Islands) and .fr (France).

Second-Level Domain Names

The second-level domain name is where your unique name or distinct brand can appear. If the second-level domain name is distinct, then the domain name may be suitable for federal trademark registration.

 ABC Printers, LLC, chose ABC.com as the domain name for the company's Web site. The second-level domain name, ABC, is the unique identifier; the gTLD, which is .com, designates ABC as a commercial entity.

Domain Names as Trademarks

There is a difference between domain names and trademarks. Domain names are unique to their owner. No two domain names are exactly the same. But they can be very similar.

 Domain names such as book.com, books.com, book-1.com, book.net, books.net, book.org, and books.org can all coexist.

On the other hand, trademark law allows two or more trademarks to exist for the same mark as long as they are in different classes.

 For the trademark E MUSE:

E MUSE – International Class 016: Newsletters and books in the field of comedy, owned by ABC Corporation.

E MUSE – International Class 042: Consulting services, namely research and presentations in the field of astrology, owned by XYZ, LLC.

To properly act as a trademark or service mark, your domain name must actually be used in connection with the associated goods or services in addition to serving as a domain name. If the domain name is used only as an Internet address, that use will not result in trademark or service mark rights. On the other hand, a mark that has been given trademark or service mark rights through actual or constructive use can be used as a domain name provided it affords a unique Internet address. For example, in BlackVoices.com™ the second level domain name, BlackVoices, is used in connection with associated services, including an online e-zine (electronic magazine), in addition to serving as the Internet address for BlackVoices.com.

The PTO will not register domain names in which the second-level name is not unique. For example, books.com, pens.com, and furniture.com could not be registered as trademarks because the words in their second-level names (books, pens, furniture) are generic.

The prefixes e- and i-, indicating electronic and Internet, are not protectable as trademarks unless the word they accompany is unique and not descriptive or generic. For example, eBook.com is a generic name for a book (not suitable for registration of any goods or services actually dealing with books); on the other hand, iUniverse.com® is unique and arbitrary terminology for a book publisher and is therefore suitable for trademark or service mark registration.

Domain Name Disputes

Domain name disputes have arisen largely from the practice of *cybersquatting*, which involves the registration of trademarks and brand names of established companies and individuals by third parties as domain names. Since registration of domain names is simple and inexpensive – usually under $40U.S. – cybersquatters use the opportunity to register hundreds of trademarks or brand names as domain names. As the holders of these domain names, cybersquatters often put them up for auction or offer them for sale directly to the company or person involved, at prices much more than the cost of domain registration. They also may keep the domain name and use the good reputation of the person or business associated with it to attract business for their own sites.

Originally there was no agreement within the Internet community that would allow organizations which register domain names to prescreen the filing of potentially problematic names. The reasons included the stimulation of business as well as First Amendment rights of freedom of expression and difficulties in determining ownership rights in a name or brand. Over time more disputes and litigation between the cybersquatters and trademark owners evolved. Today, with the new classes of top-level domains, a number of prescreening alternatives are being tested and used to discourage cyber-squatting activity.

Dispute Resolution: Two major vehicles have come into existence to settle domain name disputes: the Uniform Domain Name Dispute Resolution Policy (UDRP) and the Anticybersquatting Consumer Protection Act (ACPA).

ICANN, the organization responsible for, among other things, management of the generic top-level domains, recognized the urgent need to solve the dispute-resolution problem. A system of internationally uniform and mandatory proce-dures to deal with what are frequently disputes across borders was sought.

With the support of its member states, the World Intellectual Property Organization (WIPO), which is mandated to promote the protection of intellectual property worldwide, consulted extensively with members of the Internet community around the world. Using information from a WIPO report containing recommendations dealing with domain-name issues, ICANN adopted UDRP.

UDRP: This policy went into effect on December 1, 1999, for all ICANN-accredited registrars of Internet domain names. UDRP permits complainants to file a case with a resolution service provider, specifying

☑ the domain name in question

☑ the respondent or holder of the domain name

☑ the registrar with whom the domain name was registered

☑ the grounds for the complaint

Such grounds include, as their central criteria, the way in which the domain name is identical or similar to a trademark to which the complainant has rights; why the respondent should be considered as having no rights or legitimate interests in respect to the domain name that is the subject of the complaint; and why the domain name should be considered as having been registered and used in bad faith.

These disputes have been decided overwhelmingly in favor of the trademark holder, and thus cybersquatting has been extinguished in large part. The process is cost-efficient and quick. Legitimate questions still arise that require dispute resolution. For example, more than one person may have the same registered trademark for a different product or industry; therefore each has a legitimate right to have the domain name.

Anticybersquatting Consumer Protection Act (ACPA): On November 29, 1999, ACPA was enacted by the United States Congress and became a part of the Lanham Act. ACPA gives trademark holders greater leverage with cybersquatters and an ability to protect their interest in their trademark. ACPA has provisions for injunctive relief and statutory damages. It is another weapon to use against cybersquatters and is similar to UDRP in its effect.

Meta Tags

Meta tags are special types of HTML (HyperText Markup Language) tags that provide information about Web pages. The three particularly important meta tags are described below.

Title: The title meta tag is the short title of your Web site, which is displayed in the Web browser heading.

Description: The description meta tag is a short comment that informs search engines about what can be found at the site.

Keyword: The keyword meta tag is designed to alert Web search engines to those terms the author of the site or the webmaster considers especially important, and to draw users to the site.

Search engines such as Google, Lycos, and Yahoo! create their various indices from a review of the meta tags contained within a Web site. Therefore, Web page authors will include meta tags in the HTML and use terms, including trademarks, that they think will attract users. Webmasters often repeat keywords many times so that the search engines will rank their Web site over those of their competitors.

> Authors of Web pages will often carry the trademark of competitors in their keyword meta tags, thereby hoping to attract users who are trying to locate Web sites associated with their competitors' trademarks. Many courts have prohibited these practices.

Trademarks are valuable assets. They symbolize the goodwill that Literary Entrepreneurs have established with their customers, clients, and the marketplace at large through their goods or services. In fact, trademarks may be the

79

most valuable assets of your business. Therefore, it is critical to select, use, register, maintain, and protect your trademarks because the life of your business and your future success may depend on it.

A Brief History of Intellectual Property Law

Chapter 10

In 2002, the United States Congress noted that copyright-based industries represent one of the most valuable economic assets of this country, contributing more than 5 percent of the gross domestic product. In addition, the intellectual property sector employs approximately 4,300,000 people, representing more than 3 percent of total United States employment. Apart from their economic benefits to society, literary and artistic contributions have proved to be an integral part of individual, community, and societal success. Thus, intellectual property remains as important in today's society as it was when the drafters gathered to create the constitutional right of an author to control how his or her writings, art, or discoveries are used. This right is deeply rooted in American law. As stated in the U.S. Constitution, article I, section 8:

> The Congress shall have Power ... To promote the Progress of Science and useful Arts, by securing for limited Times to Authors and Inventors the exclusive Right to their respective Writings and Discoveries.

Copyright and trademark laws are of particular interest and concern to writers because they are integrally related to the writing process.

The History of Copyright Law

One of the first enactments of copyright law occurred on May 31, 1790. Congress has since made several substantial revisions to the law.

Act of 1909

The first major revision occurred in 1909 and was codified in 1947 as Title 17 of the Copyright Act. The 1909 act required strict adherence to the formalities of copyright notice, registration, and renewal. Therefore, works that were otherwise protectable could fall into the public domain if any of the formalities were not satisfied. The 1909 act continues to apply to works created before January 1, 1978.

> Care should be taken if a new work, otherwise governed by the Revised Act of 1976, incorporates parts of a prior work that is governed by the 1909 act.

Act of 1976

The 1909 act was substantially revised in 1976. This first version of the 1976 act (see below for the revised version) – also commonly referred to by writers and publishers as the Act of 1989 – applies to works created between January 1, 1978 and February 28, 1989, known as the Decennial Era of Copyright Law. While somewhat less stringent than the 1909 law, the 1976 act still required authors to adhere to certain formalities of notice and registration, and denied copyright protection for any works that failed to comply, moving them into the public domain.

Act of 1976 Revised

In 1989, Congress revised the 1976 act to amend certain provisions so that United States copyright law would comply with the Berne Convention for the Protection of Literary and Artistic Works. The Berne Convention is an international copyright treaty that requires all signatories to eliminate the requirements for notice and registration as a condition of copyright protection. Formalities like notice and registration are still important, however, because works created after 1978 and before 1989 are governed by the original version of the 1976 act.

One of the most prominent and important concepts recognized and pro-tected by the Berne Convention is the concept of moral rights. The term "moral rights" (or *droit moral*) encompasses the right of attribution and the right of integrity. The right of attribution ensures that artists are properly identified with the works they create and are not associated with works they did not create. The right of integrity prevents the intentional distortion, mutilation, or other modification of a work of art that injures an artist's honor or reputation.

82

Moral rights are personal to the author and therefore may not be transferred to another person. However, moral rights may be waived by a written docu-ment signed by the author. Moral rights have been recognized for many years in most European countries and in other signatory nations of the Berne Convention, but not explicitly by the United States.

When Congress amended the 1976 act, it expressly declared that the Berne Convention protections are not self-executing (not automatically incorporated by reference into U.S. law), that claims arising under the Berne Convention must be handled according to the existing laws of the United States, and that no further rights beyond those expressly included by amendment are recognized. The practical effect of these declarations was that Congress declined to adopt the moral rights provisions of the Berne Convention, stating that the rights of attribution and integrity were sufficiently protected under existing federal, state, and local laws. That conclusion was challenged and ultimately addressed, in part, in 1990.

Visual Arts Rights Act of 1990

Realizing the inconsistency between United States copyright law and the Berne Convention in regard to moral rights, Congress enacted the Visual Arts Rights Act (VARA) to grant visual artists, such as painters and sculptors, the rights of attribution and integrity for certain one-of-a-kind and limited-edition prints of visual art works.

> In the 2001 case Flack v. Friends of Queen Catherine, Inc., the federal district court in the Southern District of New York held that a grossly negligent or intentional modification of a work of visual art may be actionable under VARA.

The passage of VARA was the first instance in which the United States recognized and expressly granted moral rights, but Congress did so in a very limited way. VARA extended moral rights protection to visual artists who create paintings, drawings, limited prints, sculptures, and still photographs produced for exhibition purposes only. The Copyright Act enumerates several limitations and requirements for the work of a visual artist to enjoy the protections of moral rights. For more information about VARA, see www.copyright.gov/title17/92chap1.html#106a (general provisions) and www.copyright.gov/title17/92chap1.html#113 (scope of rights and exception for artwork incorporated into buildings).

Digital Millennium Copyright Act

Congress enacted another significant amendment to the Copyright Act, the Digital Millennium Copyright Act, in 1998, made up of the World Intellectual Property Organization (WIPO) Copyright Treaty, the WIPO Performances and Phonograms Treaty, the Online Copyright Infringement Liability Limitation Act, the Computer Maintenance Competition Assurance Act, and the Vessel Hull Design Protection Act. Specific discussion of these various acts is well beyond the scope of this book. The Digital Millennium Copyright Act, however, sought to bring the body of copyright law in line with unique technological advances like software and the Internet. As it did with the Berne Convention, Congress made it clear that WIPO was not self-executing and that no further rights were granted other than those expressly provided in the law.

The History of Trademark Law

Unlike patent and copyright law, federal trademark law has no constitutional provision that expressly permits its development. The basis for the federal trademark law is the Commerce clause in the U.S. Constitution, article I, section 8, which states in part:

> The Congress shall have the power to regulate Commerce with foreign Nations, and among the several States ...

Under the authority of the Commerce clause, Congress passed the Lanham Act (found at 15 U.S.C. § 1051 et seq.) to establish a federal system of trademark registration. Congress also decided that the Patent and Trademark Office would administer the regulation of trademarks on a national level.

The Lanham Act not only ensures the nationwide protection of trademarks but protects against deceptive practices in marketing goods and services. If you couple federal trademark law with state common law and state statutory law, you will find that you have several alternatives for registering and protecting your trademarks.

Pending Legislation Affecting Authors

Chapter 11

Bill Number	Title	Date of Introduction
H.R. 5057	Intellectual Property Protection Act of 2002	6/27/2002
H.R. 4643	Freelance Writers and Artists Protection Act of 2002	5/2/2002
S. 2395	Anti-Counterfeiting Amendments of 2002	4/30/2002
S. 2082	Playwrights Licensing Relief Act of 2002	4/10/2002
S. 2031	Intellectual Property Protection Restoration Act of 2002	3/19/2002

Intellectual Property Protection Act of 2002 (H.R. 5057)

Finding that existing law does not provide adequate civil and criminal remedies to combat tampering activities that directly facilitate counterfeiting crimes, Congressman Lamar Smith of Texas, joined by others, introduced the Intellectual Property Protection Act of 2002 (H.R. 5057) to amend the federal criminal code. The proposed amendment bans the sale of illegal authentication features, which are used to safeguard genuine copies and distinguish between legal and illegal copies, and gives copyright owners the ability to sue in civil court for monetary and other damages (see Chapter 12).

The primary purpose of H.R. 5057 is to prevent and punish counterfeiting and copyright piracy by organized criminal enterprises. Specifically, the bill seeks to curb the illegal trafficking of counterfeit labels, illicit authentication features, and counterfeit documentation or packaging on records, cassettes, CDs (sound recordings), computer programs, videos, and DVDs (audiovisual), or documentation or packaging for any of these products.

The *Congressional Record* states that while the intellectual property sector in the United States has invested millions of dollars to develop highly sophisticated authentication features to safeguard genuine intellectual property products and packaging, and to distinguish them from counterfeits, organized crime entities have invested millions of hours circumventing those safeguards.

Penalties under this proposed legislation include equitable relief, such as temporary or permanent injunctions and impounding (see Chapter 12), actual

85

damages based on the retail price of the copy times the number of copies and/or reasonable attorney fees, or statutory damages ranging from $2,500 to $25,000. Triple damages could be awarded if someone violated this provision again within three years of the last violation. A lawsuit under this section would have to be instituted within three years after the date the violation is discovered.

As of this writing, the bill awaits discussion by the Subcommittee on Courts, the Internet, and Intellectual Property.

Freelance Writers and Artists Protection Act of 2002 (H.R. 4643)

Congressman John Conyers Jr. and others introduced the Freelance Writers and Artists Protection Act of 2002 on May 2, 2002, and it was referred to the House Judiciary Committee for discussion on the same day. The bill provides for the special application of the antitrust laws to certain negotiations of freelance writers and artists for the sale of their written and graphic material to publishers.

Anti-Counterfeiting Amendments of 2002 (S. 2395)

In February 2002, Senator Joseph R. Biden held a hearing titled "Theft of American Intellectual Property: Fighting Crime Abroad and At Home." Thereafter, he issued a report on piracy against intellectual property. He noted in a speech on the Senate floor that "the current law criminalizes trafficking in counterfeit documentation and packaging, but only for software programs. The Anti-Counterfeiting Amendments of 2002 [S. 2395] update and expand these provisions to include documentation and packaging for phonorecords, motion pictures, and other audiovisual works." Senator Biden and others introduced S. 2395 on April 30, 2002. It is the Senate counterpart to H.R. 5057 discussed above. The bill was reported (officially announced) in the Senate on July 18, 2002, and placed on the Senate Legislative Calendar under General Orders.

Playwrights Licensing Relief Act of 2002 (S. 2082)

Senators Orin Hatch and Charles Schumer introduced the Playwrights Licensing Relief Act of 2002 on April 10, 2002, to modify the application of the antitrust laws to permit collective development and implementation of a standard contract form for playwrights for the licensing of their plays. When Senator Hatch introduced the bill, he explained the intent of the legislation as follows: "I am proud that this legislation enables playwrights to act collectively without violating the antitrust laws. It lets them develop standard form contracts as well as provisions ensuring that certain artists' rights are respected in the production of their plays. These steps will help support playwrights, especially young playwrights, as they enter this increasingly sophisticated and consolidated market. By helping playwrights in [this] way we encourage the continued vibrance of our American theater and culture." This bill was referred to the Judiciary Committee.

Intellectual Property Protection Restoration Act of 2002 (S. 2031)

On March 19, 2002, Senators Patrick Leahy and Sam Brownback introduced the Intellectual Property Protection Restoration Act of 2002 (S. 2031) to restore federal remedies for infringements of intellectual property by states. Currently, states enjoy sovereign immunity, meaning they cannot be sued for infringements of intellectual property although they can own such property and sue to protect their own rights.

Senator Leahy explained in the *Congressional Record* that S. 2031 "creates reasonable incentives for States to waive their sovereign immunity in intellectual property cases. States that choose not to waive their immunity within 2 years after enactment would continue to enjoy many of the benefits in the intellectual property marketplace. However, like private parties that sue States for infringement, States that sue private parties for infringement will not be able to recover any money damages unless they waive their immunity from liability in intellectual property cases. All other remedial actions will continue to be available to State litigants."

Absent this legislation, Senators Leahy and Brownback assert, states will continue to enjoy the unfair advantage of avoiding money damages when they infringe the rights of private parties, while remaining free to obtain money damages when their own rights are infringed. This reality, the sponsors state, "discourage[s] technological innovation and artistic creation, and compromise[s] the ability of the United States to advocate effective enforcement of intellectual property rights in other countries and to fulfill its own obligations under international treaties." Their point is well made since the United States is one of the leading voices for intellectual property protection throughout the world. Therefore, the sponsors believe that the United States cannot be inconsistent in its own protection of intellectual property rights by giving states a free pass to avoid infringement liability and at the same time enjoy the legal benefits of owning intellectual property.

Contracts Basics
Chapter 12

Every contract, whether written or oral, includes three basic elements: the offer, the acceptance, and the consideration.

A contract is a legally enforceable agreement between two or more legally competent parties – individuals, businesses, or other organizations – in which one party makes an offer to do or refrain from doing something, the other accepts the offer, and each exchanges something of value, also called consideration. Consideration is a legal concept best described as the benefit or detriment that induces someone to make a promise and enter into a contractual arrangement based on the terms, conditions, rights, and obligations agreed to by the parties involved.

Contracts are legally enforceable only if there is sufficient consideration to show that each party has given something of value to benefit from the deal. For example, if A offers to print B's books for $2,000, and B accepts by giving A $2,000 for the printed books, and A gives B the printed books, each gives something of value.

By contrast, an offer and acceptance without adequate consideration is merely a gift. For instance, if A offers to give B $10, and B accepts but makes no promise in return, then A's transfer of $10 to B is a gift and not a legally enforceable contract. The practical effect is that generally speaking, B cannot sue A to pay the $10 if A reneges on her promise. But in some cases a court will enforce an agreement made for less than adequate consideration if one party relied to his or her disadvantage on the promise of another. This is known in legalese as detrimental reliance.

A contract is void if the promise on which it is based is illegal or illicit. For example, an agreement between two drug dealers about the exchange of money for drugs is not legally enforceable because the promises involve the completion of an illegal act.

A valid contract must contain the material terms – the most important terms – of the agreement: the who, what, where, when, and how of the mutual benefits and obligations. Collectively, these essential terms will govern the transaction.

???? If it's not in writing, it's not a legally enforceable contract.

This assumption is false. An oral agreement can be enforceable in court if the basic contract elements exist and the essential terms are mutually agreed upon. But certain contracts are legally required to be in writing. Contracts are governed by state law, which of course differs from state to state. Nonetheless, each state has a Statute of Frauds which requires that certain contracts be in writing. In most cases, the following contracts must be in writing:

☑ wills

☑ sale of real property

☑ lease of property with a term of more than one year

☑ contracts with a term of more than one year or a value above a certain amount

Nonetheless, to be prudent, it is best to put all agreements in writing to have records of them and to avoid misunderstandings and miscommunications.

Breach of Contract and Damages

When one party fails to perform his or her obligations under the contract, this is known as a breach of the contract, and the non-breaching party may sue to enforce the terms of the contract and collect damages (although there are other remedies short of filing a lawsuit that may be effective). The premise of damages is to make the non-breaching party "whole," that is, restored to his or her position before entering into the agreement. This premise is different from criminal penalties that seek to punish and to reform behavior.

In most cases, the non-breaching party will receive monetary damages. Sometimes, however, money will not make the non-breaching party whole. For example, when an author licenses her article to a magazine for first serial print publication rights, but the publisher also posts the article on its Web site without obtaining electronic rights, the author may sue for monetary damages (statutory damages if he or she was savvy enough to have registered the copyright within three months of publication). But the author may also not want the article posted online for a variety of reasons. In fact, getting the magazine to remove the article from its Web site may be more valuable to the author than any amount of money he or she may be entitled to recover. Therefore, the author may, in addition to money damages, demand equitable damages in the form of an injunction to force the magazine publisher to remove the article from the Web site.

The following are the various damages and other remedies available:

☑ **Compensatory Damages:** Money damages to compensate the non-breaching party for the amount of the loss

☞ **Consequential and Incidental Damages:** Additional money damages to compensate the non-breaching party for other costs associated with the breach that were reasonably anticipated (even if not actually anticipated) by all parties when they entered the contract

☞ **Attorney Fees and Costs:** Recovery of the costs of litigation by the non-breaching party if included in the terms of the contract

☞ **Liquidated Damages:** Monetary damages expressly provided for in the terms of the contract; usually included when actual monetary damages would be difficult to determine if a breach occurred

☞ **Specific Performance:** A court order for the breaching party to perform as agreed to in the contract; not applicable to contracts to sing or write, for instance, because this requirement would in effect be indentured servitude (working against one's will); but may be ordered by a court to transfer unique property

☞ **Punitive Damages:** Money awarded only in the most egregious cases to deter the breaching party and others from repeated occurrences of the wrongdoing; almost never awarded in contract cases

☞ **Rescission:** When the contract is terminated and both parties are excused from further performance

☞ **Reformation:** When the contract is revised to properly reflect the original intentions of the parties

Defenses to a Claim of Breach of Contract

Even where breach of contract is established, a defendant may avoid liability by proving at least one of the most common legal defenses:

☞ **Lack of Consideration:** At least one party did not give something of value to the other party. As a result the transfer is considered a gift instead of a legally enforceable contract.

☞ **Duress, Undue Influence, Fraud:** One party was under significant pressure (give me your money, or I'll kill you) or was tricked into signing the contract.

☞ **Lack of Competence:** One of the contracting parties was a minor (minors cannot enter into contracts) or was mentally incapable of entering into a legally enforceable contract.

☞ **Impossibility:** Through no fault of either party, something unforeseeable, such as an act of God, terror, or war, occurred that made it impossible to perform under the terms of the contract.

☞ **Illegality:** The terms of the contract were illegal, making the contract legally unenforceable.

91

The Publishing Agreement
Chapter 13

In simple terms, a publishing agreement 📄 (also referred to as a book deal or contract) is a legal arrangement between an author and publisher. The author agrees to transfer to the publisher certain rights in the bundle of rights associated with her copyrighted manuscript, and the publisher agrees, in turn, to pay for the costs to publish the manuscript. In exchange, both parties receive some financial gain (the publisher reaping the lion's share, of course). Basically, the publisher is an investor in the author's manuscript – the publisher agrees to pay for all costs of publishing (in the best-case scenario). In exchange, the publisher is entitled to recoup the initial investment and to take a sizeable percentage of the income generated by sales and licensing of the work. The author often receives an advance against royalties (explained below) and a percentage of royalties and subsidiary rights income.

Many complaints are hurled at publishers for the seemingly unfair percentages of income and the extensive rights they retain in publishing deals. But the publishing industry, like any industry, is very much a bottom-line business. And it is often a challenge for publishers to make profits, since the majority of publishing agreements do not earn out, meaning that most publishers (small and big alike) do not earn back their initial investment, which includes the author's advance. This advance is a payment to the author before publication; it is offset by income from sales after publication; in other words, it's a loan from the publisher to the author.

Generally, publishers create a profit and loss statement to anticipate the costs of publication (prepress, printing, marketing, and promotion) and projected earnings, in light of the proposed market and demand for the book, industry discounts of at least 50 percent, and returns of at least 20 percent. Based on the net profit number, the publisher selects a figure it reasonably believes it will recoup from sales and, in most cases, pays the author an advance based on some percentage of that anticipated profit. A book earns out when all costs, including the advance, are recouped from sales and licensing revenue.

But it is not uncommon for a book to go out of print after selling only five thousand copies. Imagine the following scenario: You sign an agreement with a major publishing company in New York for hardcover rights to your fiction manuscript. You receive a modest $60,000 advance and a standard royalty schedule of 10 percent for the first five thousand copies sold. If the net retail price is $24.95, gross profit on 5,000 copies would be $124,750. Apply an average industry discount of 50 percent and net profits are reduced to $62,375. Now apply the loss of income for returns of 20 percent and the net profits are reduced to $49,900. Subtract $20,000 in production costs (not including your advance) and $29,900 remains. Your royalty of 10 percent yields $2,990, against which your author advance is applied and the publisher is still in the hole to recoup the remaining $57,010 paid in advance to you.

But do not cry for the publisher just yet because it does pocket $26,910. In addition, the example does not account for the licensing of subsidiary rights like book club rights, mass market rights, audio book rights, electronic rights, and so forth. The point is that the publishing industry is a dollars-and-cents business from the publisher's perspective. And despite your core values as a creative spirit who values words over profits, if you intend to be successful in this business, you must begin to understand and embrace the bottom line too.

Why You Need a Written Contract

It is critical to put the agreement between author and publisher in writing because the terms and conditions determine what rights are transferred, what compensation you and the publisher receive, when the rights revert back to you, and what state law governs the contract if a disagreement develops. You should never leave these issues to oral agreements or handshake deals. Always get it in writing and make sure the contract states clearly what each party agrees to do and what each will receive in return.

Now hear this, authors: You do a disservice to yourself, given your hard work and considerable talents, when you dot every "i" and cross every "t" in your manuscript but rush through a publishing agreement, often without the guidance of an experienced literary lawyer, and sign it without negotiating the terms from a position of knowledge and strength. Or worse yet, you fail to ensure that all material terms are negotiated favorably and stated clearly in a written agreement signed by you and the publisher.

In the days and weeks leading up to the signing of a publishing agreement you are in the strongest position from which to negotiate. And this time is the most important because your contract defines what rights you are transferring, what (if any) rights you keep, how your agent and publisher get paid, and how you get paid. Keep in mind that what you agree to today affects you and the other party or parties for years to come. Don't you think that is worth taking seriously and slowly?

Consider this: although a certain author advance and royalty schedule may seem great now, how fair will it be when you are a best-selling author yet still earning pennies on each book sold while the publisher has long since recouped its investment and is still raking in the lion's share of the profits? Or perhaps transferring all of your rights to a publisher may seem like a good idea now. But what if the publisher does not have any intention of using some of the rights or is actually in no better position than you to properly exploit them? Why transfer them in the first place? This is especially true since it may be more financially beneficial to divide the rights and sell them to a number of different buyers than to lump them together and sell to one buyer.

The point is that there is no such thing as a nonnegotiable contract. Do not sign a contract with anyone who tells you there is. Everything is up for discussion. Compare this process to other areas of your life and ask yourself, "Would I just sign *any* paper given to me if I were buying a house or car, or making a long-term investment, or going into a long-term business relationship with someone I just met?" We venture to guess that your answer to these questions would be no, and that you would take care to read the document and consult with someone more knowledgeable than you to make sure the rights and responsibilities of both parties were set forth clearly and that you were getting not only what is fair but what is in your best interest, to the greatest extent possible.

95

The most common fear authors have when faced with a deal is the dreaded *fear of negotiation*. In the spirit of not wanting to offend, many authors in first-time bargaining situations shy away from asking hard questions and requesting more favorable provisions. Worse still, some authors are intimidated by the process and the documents. That, coupled with an author's excitement over the possibility of *any* deal, after receiving so many rejections, is a dangerous mix that often spells trouble. Authors do not want to challenge the agent or publisher because they do not want to be perceived as difficult or money hungry. But remember, this is a bottom-line business, and the operative word is business. Agents and publishers have their own attorneys, and so should you. Any reputable person in the industry understands that offers should be negotiated by competent professionals; it's just business.

The Contract Terms

There are as many variations in the precise terms of a publishing agreement as there are publishing agreements. But certain key terms should exist in every contract. This section focuses on key clauses in a standard publishing agreement. You will find a complete sample form in Appendix B and in the Forms Library on the CD.

Understanding the nature, purpose, meaning, and effect of the key clauses in the contract is an important first step in breaking down complex legal terminology into common understanding. Of course, literary law is a vast and complex subject. Accordingly, this section is merely a broad overview of some of the most common and essential clauses in a publishing agreement. Compare the discussion that follows to the corresponding clause in the sample contract.

Introductory Paragraph: Most contracts begin with an introductory paragraph that sets forth the names and legal capacities of the parties as well as the effective date of the agreement. It may also include their addresses.

> ☉━🗝 This Agreement is made this _____ day of _____, 2003 (The Agreement), by and between _____, an individual (hereinafter referred to as AUTHOR) located at _____, and ABC Publishing Company, a corporation (hereinafter referred to as PUBLISHER) whose principal place of business is located at _____, concerning a work presently entitled _____ (as described in greater detail below).

Description of the Work: The Description of the Work clause, although simple to understand, is a clause to which you should pay close attention. In many cases the description is basic and general, providing an approximate page length or a specified number of words, the general topic, and the tentative title. But you should consider including more information or incorporating the book proposal and/or sample chapters as an attachment (known as an Exhibit) to the agreement. This revision is important to consider if the publisher has the right to reject the manuscript and terminate the agreement if it is not "acceptable to the publisher in form and content" (see "Delivery" and "Acceptance" sections below). If the publisher has this right to reject, you need to be reasonably certain that your understanding of what the manuscript will contain is consistent with the publisher's expectation of what you will submit. Problems can result when the publisher's expectations for the manuscript differ from the author's understanding. Therefore, sometimes a more detailed description benefits both parties.

©🔑 Delivery and Acceptance of the Manuscript

Author shall deliver to Publisher on or before _____, 2003 (the Delivery Date), one (l) original hardcopy of the complete Work and one (l) copy on computer disk, together with any supplementary materials (including, without limitation, drawings, illustrations, photographs, maps, graphs, tables). If Author fails to deliver the Work by the delivery date, after a thirty (30) day grace period (or such other time period as shall be determined by the Publisher and agreed to in writing by both parties), Publisher may demand the return of all sums paid to or on behalf of Author by Publisher in connection with the Work, and this Agreement shall terminate. Upon termination under these circumstances, Author may not resubmit the Work (or any part thereof) or a similar work to any other publisher without first offering it to Publisher under the same terms contained in this Agreement.

Publisher shall inform the Author in writing as to whether the complete Work is acceptable to Publisher in form and content within ninety (90) days of receipt of the complete Work. If Publisher determines the Work is unacceptable but capable of cure, Publisher and Author shall agree upon a time for revision (Revision Period) and Publisher shall provide to Author written comments explaining the necessary revisions. If Publisher determines that the first submission cannot be cured or that the revision created during the Revision Period is still unacceptable, Publisher shall have the right, in Publisher's sole discretion, to reject the Work by giving written notice to the Author.

If the Work is rejected, Author shall keep fifty percent (50%) of the advances paid to date and shall return the remaining fifty percent (50%) within one year of rejection. The Author may submit the Work to a third party, provided that Author shall remain obligated to repay to Publisher the amounts retained by Author from all proceeds from any sale of license by the Author of rights of any nature in the Work to a third party (the First Proceeds).

The clauses dealing with delivery and acceptance of the manuscript are important and sometimes problematic parts of the contract.

97

Delivery: The contract should spell out the date that the manuscript is due and in what form it should be delivered (hardcopy, diskette, or both), as well as any technical specifications (margins, one-sided, double-spaced) required by the publisher. In addition, any supplementary materials expected to accompany the manuscript (photographs, illustrations, and other materials created by someone else – that may require permissions) should be noted in this section.

🔲 Supplementary Materials and Indexing

Be sure to check the fine print in the contract about supplementary materials (photographs, illustrations, artwork, interview excerpts, and so forth). If supplementary materials are included in your work, a publisher will require that you get permission from the owner to include them in your work. Also, if you transferred to an agent rights that you intend to give to the publisher, you will need permission from the agent to do so (often covered by an agency clause inserted into the contract). Lastly, if your work needs an index, the publisher will require either that you provide it when you deliver your complete manuscript (or sometime thereafter as agreed to) or that you pay for the expense of having the index written.

First, confirm whether you are responsible for (1) obtaining and (2) paying for supplementary materials. Generally publishers require in the contract that authors seek and pay for the cost of obtaining permissions, although sometimes the publisher will agree to actually obtain permission since it may be in a better position to do so. Publishers will also ask you to pay for illustrations, artwork, maps, indexing, and so forth. But these requirements can (and should) be negotiated so that either the publisher pays or the costs are split between publisher and author. If you cannot change the terms, try to get the publisher to advance you the money and to recoup its expenses from your royalty account so that you do not have to pay any out-of-pocket expenses.

For a sample permission form, see Appendix B.

Acceptance: At times a publisher or an editor at a large publishing company will offer a book deal in response to a query letter, proposal, or pitch. Based on that material, the editor will formulate certain expectations of the final manuscript. If those expectations are not adequately spelled out in writing and conveyed to the author, the finished product will not be what the editor expected.

Another possibility is that although the editor conveys his or her expectations clearly, the author, who was great at crafting a pitch, is ill equipped to finish the manuscript. To deal with these contingencies, publishers often demand that the manuscript be delivered in form and content satisfactory to the publisher. Clearly, this is subjective and gives a publisher wide latitude to reject a manuscript. Some authors negotiate for a more objective clause that sets forth criteria that, if met, will render the manuscript fit for publication. An alternate approach is to give the author the opportunity to cure the defect (revise the manuscript) based on the publisher's comments.

⊙━🔑 Grant of Rights

The Author hereby grants, transfers, and assigns to the Publisher for the full term of copyright the exclusive right to publish in hardback and paperback editions (the Primary Rights) and sell throughout the world in the English language the literary work presently entitled _____

98

(hereinafter called Work). **The Author also grants and assigns to the Publisher the exclusive subsidiary rights to said literary Work, with exclusive authority to license said rights in all countries and in all languages.**

This clause defines the rights the author will assign to the publisher, the nature of the rights, the applicable territory, and the amount of time the contract will remain in effect (but see the section "Reclaiming Your Copyright after Transfer" in Chapter 2). The assignment of rights means that the publisher and not the author is the owner of whatever rights are conveyed during the term of the agreement. Generally, the grant of rights is exclusive to one publisher. Sometimes authors assign the entire bundle of rights by way of a broad, all-inclusive grant of rights, such as the one noted in the sample clause, but you need not transfer all of your rights to the publisher. And you should always include a reservation-of-rights clause after the grant of rights as follows:

    All rights not expressly granted to the Publisher are hereby reserved by the Author.

Keep in mind that if you have or intend to have a Web site in the future, you should consider reserving rights in your domain name, and protecting your ability to sell author copies (watch for a clause that restricts your ability to sell author copies) and to provide information from your Web site with no limitation by or compensation to the publisher.

In addition, you should only grant to a publisher the rights you believe the publisher is capable of exploiting to your benefit. A publisher may, as a matter of course, seek to control all rights. However, why grant motion picture or dramatic rights, for instance, if the publisher has neither successfully exploited those rights in the past nor has established relationships in those fields to exploit the rights successfully in the future. Although licensing motion picture or dramatic rights is speculative in most cases, it may be best to retain them and sell them to others who are in a better position to successfully exploit them. The point is, do not just go along simply for the sake of appearing agreeable. And even if you cannot negotiate to keep certain sub-rights, you can use them as a bargaining chip to negotiate other clauses to your advantage.

Some authors negotiate a more limited grant of rights for a particular work (for example, the hardcover rights, paperback rights, mass market rights, book club rights, foreign rights, large print rights, and a host of others). Doing so allows the author to shop the remaining rights and negotiate a deal (based on

99

the strength of the first edition) with the same publisher or with a different one. The grant of rights can also be limited by language (for example, the English-speaking market) or by territory (North America only, for example).

Secondary (or Subsidiary) Rights: Ordinarily, the primary right granted to a book publisher is the right to publish the manuscript in book form. This right can include all print rights or, for instance, only hardback, trade paper, or mass market rights. However, some publishers seek electronic, spoken-word edition, Internet, audio, and book club rights in the primary grant. Traditionally, these rights were considered subsidiary or secondary to the primary right to publish the manuscript in book form. But as new media are developed and used to publish works in other forms, publishers will be more aggressive in attempting to control all known and future uses. Case law, however, suggests that unless the rights are expressly stated, they will not be transferred, which runs contrary to the "future media" clause in most publishing agreements.

You (or your agent, if you've transferred the rights to the agent) may also assign secondary or subsidiary rights to the publisher so that the publisher can exploit the Work in ways that may be less important (but still valuable) to the publisher, such as mass market paperback rights, book club rights, and foreign and translation rights, and in media *other than* books, such as motion picture and television rights, stage plays (dramatic rights), electronic rights, performance rights, and more. Again, keep in mind that any of these rights could be included in the primary rights clause if the publisher primarily intends to exploit them. Therefore the subsidiary rights list below is not etched in stone but a guide for your information.

Subsidiary rights include

☑ Periodical rights (first and/or second serial)

☑ Book club rights

☑ Dramatic rights (theatrical rights)

☑ Motion picture and TV rights

☑ Videocassette and audiocassette rights

☑ Radio rights

☑ Merchandising (commercial tie-in) rights

☑ New technology

☑ Foreign translation rights

☑ Electronic rights

☑ Internet rights

☑ Mass market paperback rights

One of the most important sections of a publishing contract deals with how you get paid. A publishing company can compensate an author in several different ways; sometimes the publisher uses one particular method of payment, and other times two or more methods are combined.

Advance: A more apt title for this clause would be "loan" because, as the word suggests and as stated above, this payment is an advance against future royalties. The advance is commonly paid in three installments, one-third on signing, one-third on delivery, and one-third on acceptance (or publication), although there are several variations on this theme, including half on signing and half on publication.

Royalties: Royalties are payments made by the publisher to the author based on money received from sales. Think of a royalty as a percentage of every book sale. Royalties do not ordinarily include monies earned from licensing agreements for the exploitation of subsidiary rights, as defined above.

Royalties are generally based on the retail price of the book. Royalty calculations can include escalations that attach higher rates to greater numbers of books sold. Additionally, some publishers opt to have separate royalty calculations for different editions. Typical escalations based on the U.S. cover price may look like this:

Hardback	**Trade Paper**	**Mass Market Paperback**
10% on first 5,000	7½% on first 10,000	6 to 8% on first 150,000 copies
12½% on next 5,000	10% on all add'l copies	8 to 10% on all additional copies
15% on all add'l copies		

101

Traditionally, publishers base the royalty rate on the retail or cover price. This is the price printed on the book. However, a significant number of publishers have moved away from tradition and instead base royalty rates on the net price, which is the price actually received by the publisher. This break in tradition has occurred because of the rise of mandatory discounts within the industry to booksellers (20 to 40 percent), distributors (50 to 55 percent), and wholesalers and book clubs (as much as 60 percent).

Try to secure a bonus structure for receiving what we call professional recognition. Professional recognition can be placement on a prominent best-seller list (*New York Times*), a literary prize that ultimately increases sales (Pulitzer), or any other honor, award, or achievement, such as signing a motion picture or TV deal.

Net Revenues: Sometimes publishers offer a percentage of net revenues instead of a sales royalty and licensing percentage scheme. This is most likely to be offered by independent publishers, who try to avoid the administrative hassles that accompany complex royalty calculations. Instead, the publisher will recoup its expenses and then split the remaining revenue based on a negotiated percentage.

Flat Rate: Although this is not a common option, some publishers offer a flat fee to purchase your manuscript. This may occur, for instance, in writing competitions where the prize is a lump sum plus publication.

Options: The options clause gives the publisher the first right to purchase (or refuse) the next work created by the author. A typical options clause might look like this:

> Publisher shall have the right to acquire Author's next book-length work on terms to be mutually agreed upon by the parties. Author shall submit a detailed outline and sample chapter of the next book-length work to Publisher before submitting the work to any other publisher, and Publisher shall have a period of thirty days after receipt of said detailed outline and sample chapter (the Option Period) in which to review the submission and determine whether to exercise the option. The Option Period shall not begin to run earlier than sixty days after publication of the Work. If Publisher declines or fails to exercise its option by the expiration of the Option Period, then Author may submit the work to other publishers or otherwise dispose of the work, at Author's sole discretion.

Note that in the example the publisher has the right to purchase the next work on terms "to be mutually agreed upon by the parties." But most option clauses will state that the publisher can acquire the next work on the same terms as the existing agreement. If that is the case, the same option clause (and advance and royalty rates) will appear in the second contract and the third and so on, until the publisher decides not to exercise its option. So the two-book deal winds up being a multiple-book deal for the publisher, without an opportunity for the author to negotiate a more favorable deal based on success of the first or second book.

The Court in *Pelican Publishing Co. v. Justin Wilson* held that the options clause must be drafted carefully and precisely to avoid being deemed unenforceable due to vagueness.

Of course the publisher wants as many opportunities as possible not only to recoup its sizable investment but also to benefit financially from the success of the work. On the other hand, you want to be in the position to negotiate a more lucrative and favorable deal if the initial work is successful. Therefore, this is an extremely important clause that should be negotiated carefully and comprehensively.

A sub-rights compensation clause could look like this:

The net revenues received from the exploitation of the enumerated subsidiary rights shall be shared fifty percent (50%) to the Author and fifty percent (50%) to the Publisher, except that the division of the net revenues from dramatic, motion picture, and television licenses shall be seventy-five percent (75%) to the Author and twenty-five (25%) to the Publisher.

Revisions: The revisions clause is not appropriate for fiction, but appears for most nonfiction books. At first glance, many authors are put off by the revisions clause. But in reality, revising nonfiction keeps the information fresh and can extend the shelf life of the work. But you must take care to limit the revisions clause and to insert some protective provisions that seem to be conspicuously absent from most publishing agreement drafts (to the great detriment of the author). Those provisions appear in bold in the box below.

The Author shall revise the Work (a Revised Work) **two (2) times** after initial publication and within one (1) year upon the receipt of written request from the Publisher to do so. A Revised Work shall not substantially alter the original Work and further, **shall not constitute a new work for copyright and royalty escalation purposes.** In the event that the Author is unable or unwilling to provide a revision within one (1) year after the Publisher has requested it, or should the Author be deceased, the Publisher may have the revision made **at the Publisher's expense** (such expense to be recoupable from royalties) and may display, in the revised Work and in advertising, the name of the person or persons who perform the revision.

103

This clause, as drafted, builds in certain protections for authors. First, it limits the number of revisions. Second, it states that a revision will not be considered a new work for purposes of copyright term and royalty escalations. Authors do not want the term or number of books sold to begin from zero again.

Third, authors should try to negotiate to have the publisher pay for the costs of revisions if the author does not or cannot revise the work when requested to do so.

Out-of-Print/Termination Clause: The out-of-print clause is extremely important for several reasons. First, the definition of the term "out-of-print" determines when the rights revert back to the author. Second, because of electronic publishing, including e-books, print-on-demand technology, online services, and interactive media, it can now be argued that the work will never go out of print because the electronic files and print-on-demand technology are not capable of being exhausted. Therefore, a new definition of out-of-print must be included in publishing agreements (many of which are outdated because they are used over and over again without being updated to reflect current times) today to account for these new technologies and to protect authors.

The Work shall be considered to be out of print if it is not available in the U.S. through regular retail channels in the English language book form edition and not listed in the publisher's catalog; further availability through print-on-demand or other electronic or mechanical means alone does not make a book in print. In the event that the Publisher fails to keep the Work in print and the Author makes a written request of the Publisher to keep the Work in print, the Publisher shall, within sixty (60) days after receipt of said written request, notify the Author in writing of the Publisher's decision in the matter. If the Publisher elects to keep the Work in print, it shall have six (6) months thereafter to reprint and release the Work into ordinary sales channels. In the event that the Publisher elects not to keep the Work in print or fails to comply with the six (6) month deadline (unless the failure is due to circumstances beyond its control), then this agreement shall terminate and all rights granted to the Publisher shall revert immediately to the Author.

Special clause to address electronic versions of the Work

If Publisher sells no more than _____ copies of Author's Work in either electronic or downloadable format, or by means of print-on-demand technology, over any _____ consecutive month period of this Agreement, then either party may terminate this Agreement upon thirty (30) days' notice in writing sent to the other party. Upon such termination, all rights granted under this Agreement, except the rights to dispose of existing stock, including but not limited to printed, audio, or CD-ROM copies, shall revert to Author, subject to all rights that may have been granted by Publisher to third parties under this Agreement, and Publisher shall have no further obligations or liabilities to Author except that Author's earned royalties shall be paid when and as due.

A Publisher's Duty To Publish: A publisher's duty to publish must be specifically addressed in the agreement. This includes what damages the author will receive if the publisher fails to publish as promised. The court in *Alternative Thinking Systems Inc. v. Simon & Schuster* suggested that authors should receive, at a minimum, all advances paid to date and immediate reversion of rights. What would happen if the author has not received an advance remains an unanswered question.

Publishing Agreement Checklist: A comprehensive publishing agreement will have all thirty of the following clauses:

☑ Recitation

☑ Grant of Rights, including

   Description of the Work and Rights Granted

   Territory

   Language

   Term

☑ Reservation of Rights

☑ Delivery and Acceptance of Work

☑ Additional Materials

☑ Permissions

☑ Representations and Warranties

☑ Duty to Publish

☑ Artistic Control

☑ Compensation Scheme (advance, royalties, net revenues, etc.)

☑ Subsidiary Rights

☑ Payments

☑ Accounting

☑ Inspection of Books

☑ Copyright

☑ Indemnity

☑ Free Copies

☑ Revisions

☑ Reversion

☑ Remaindering

105

☑ Successors and Assigns

☑ Termination

☑ Agent Clause (if author has an agent)

☑ Promotion/Use of Author's Persona & Likeness

☑ Arbitration

☑ Notice

☑ Entire Agreement

☑ Waiver and Default

☑ Governing Law

☑ Signature Lines

Other Important Agreements

Chapter 14

Although the publishing agreement usually receives a lot of attention, you should be aware, as a Literary Entrepreneur, that other contracts relating to the publishing industry may also be significant for you. In fact, before entering into a publishing agreement with you, a publisher may ask you for copies of a collaboration agreement (if you worked with others to create your book) and a licensing agreement (if you have incorporated the work of others – pictures, illustrations, photographs, and so forth – in your book).

The Collaboration Agreement

Although the writer's life is often solitary, sometimes two or more people decide to contribute to one work. This situation can be a blessing or a curse depending on how you set up your professional relationship with your collaborators; so if you intend to work with someone else to create a joint work, you should consider entering into a collaboration agreement.

A collaboration agreement ▣ is used when two or more people contribute to a book; the contributors may be, for example, two authors or an author and an illustrator. The collaboration agreement sets forth the understanding between the parties involved regarding the nature of the work, their business relationship, what they will each contribute, what percentage of revenue for the book each will receive, and so forth. The agreement should

- ☑ describe the work

- ☑ describe each person's contribution, the schedule of anticipated due dates, the form in which the contribution should be submitted, and the arrangements regarding how the contributors will share all financial and other responsibilities to develop the work

- ☑ state how long the collaboration agreement will remain in effect and, if the term expires or the contract is terminated, which, if any, clauses will remain in effect

- ☑ outline what happens if one of the contributors should become physically or mentally incapacitated or die during the term of the agreement

☑ set forth how artistic decisions will be made, namely, whether each contributor shares artistic control over the entire project, whether each person has individual control over his or her contribution, or whether one person has the final say about all such decisions

☑ state how business decisions will be made, namely, whether all contributors have a say, whether there will be a majority vote, or whether one contributor controls all business decisions

☑ describe what happens if or when offered an agency or publishing agreement (to the extent the contributors do not have an agent or the publishing agreement isn't already entered into)

☑ discuss how and when intellectual property rights will be applied for and/or registered

☑ address how derivative works will be managed

☑ enumerate what financial investment each party will make, whether expenses and investments will be recoupable and how revenues will be divided, and whether contributors receive income individually or one person collects on behalf of everyone and then distributes payments

☑ set forth how contributors will be credited in the work and in advertisements and publicity related to the work

☑ address the circumstances under which the agreement can be terminated

☑ declare what law shall apply in the case of a dispute and whether the parties must submit to arbitration

☑ include any other provisions that further define the rights and responsibilities of the contributors

108   The Licensing Agreement

A licensing agreement 🗎 sets forth terms that permit others the limited right to use your work. In contrast to an assignment (such as that in a publishing contract) where you, as the copyright owner, actually transfer the copyright to a new owner (the publisher), in a license you retain the copyright but give permission to the licensee to use the work in a certain way, for a certain time period, and in a specified area.

The license should

☑ describe with great specificity the property to be licensed

☑ note the date the property will be delivered to the licensee and in what form it must be delivered

☑ describe with great specificity the rights granted to the licensee, namely, setting forth exactly how the licensee is allowed to use the property and whether those rights are exclusive or nonexclusive

☑ note the language and geographical locations in which the property can be used and how long the license will remain in effect

☑ include a reservation-of-rights clause stating that any use not expressly granted in the license is reserved by you

☑ set forth the payment terms, which may include a lump sum license fee, advance, royalty schedule, license fees paid in installments, and so forth

☑ include provisions for copyright notice and credit

☑ address whether the licensee has the right to alter the property in any way

☑ include a confidentiality clause for any proprietary information disclosed to the licensee regarding the property or your business pursuits

☑ outline the ways each party can terminate the agreement

☑ discuss whether parties must submit to arbitration in case of a dispute

☑ discuss whether the license can be assigned by any party

☑ include the governing law

☑ include a no-agency clause

You should make sure that the license is comprehensive enough to secure rights in all intended uses. The *New York Times, Newsday*, and *Time Magazine* (print publishers) and NEXIS and University Microfilms International (UMI) (electronic publishers) learned this lesson the hard way. On June 25, 2001, in *New York Times et al. v. Tasini et al.*, the Supreme Court in a seven-to-two decision upheld the rights of Jonathan Tasini, Mary Kay Blakely, Barbara Garson, Margot Mifflin, Sonia Jaffe Robbins, and David S. Whitford, all freelance writers, to require the print and online publishers involved to acquire the right to include their copyrighted works in electronic databases that store information in a text-only format.

The authors, all of whom worked as independent contractors, individually transferred to at least one of the print publishers first serial rights in his or her article to be included in a collective work (the newspaper or magazine). The publishers licensed the text of articles appearing in their publications to NEXIS – and the *Times* (but not *Newsday* or *Time*) also licensed *Times* materials to

UMI to reproduce those materials on two CD-ROM products – to include in the electronic database. Through a computerized retrieval system, database users sign on to their account (or access the CD-ROM), and search the database for files by author, subject, date, publication, headline, key term, words in text, or other criteria. In response to the input information, the search agent scans the database and provides the user with a list of all the articles that meet the search criteria. The user can view, print, or download the individual articles, which are displayed with information about the print publication, publication date, section, initial page number, headline or title, and author. But individual articles are not linked to the other articles with which they appeared in the collective work; rather, each stands alone. The authors registered their individual copyrights and the publishers registered their copyrights in their collective works.

The writers alleged in their original complaint that their copyrights had been infringed by the inclusion of their articles in the databases, and they sought declaratory and injunctive relief, and monetary damages. In response, the publishers argued that they were entitled to reproduce and distribute the articles because of the privilege given to collective-work copyright owners.

The Court disagreed with the publishers and concluded that the databases could not be considered collective works because the articles stood alone rather than in the context of the entire work (magazine or newspaper) or any revision of the work (a special edition), or even as a later work within the same series (a "where are they now" piece). Thus the Court ruled that the publishers infringed the copyrights of the freelance authors.

There are many critical points in *Tasini*; however, as it pertains to licensing agreements, the ruling demonstrates that the electronic publishers believed they had the right to use the literary property transferred from the print publishers. In fact they did not. In retrospect, of course, the electronic publishers should have required the print publishers to attach the necessary permissions to use the individual works. As you can see, the expense of not getting the proper permissions to use copyrighted work turned out to be far greater than that of obtaining the permissions beforehand.

Resources For Writers

Appendix A

Resource	Contact
Web Sites	
Copyright Clearance Center	www.copyright.com, not to be confused with copyright.gov (the official Copyright Office Web site listed below)
Copyright Office	www.copyright.gov
FindLaw.com: an online database of helpful legal resources for many different areas of the law	www.FindLaw.com
Intellectual Property Owners Association	www.ipo.org
Internet Corporation for Assigned Names and Numbers (ICANN)	www.icann.org
Legal Information Institute of Cornell University	www.law.cornell.edu
Library of Congress	www.loc.gov
United States Patent and Trademark Office	www.uspto.gov
World Intellectual Property Organization (WIPO): an international organization focused on protecting the rights of intellectual property owners	www.wipo.org

Conferences

Black Writers Reunion and Conference	www.blackwriters.org/conference/index.html
BookExpo America	www.bookexpoamerica.com
Frankfurt Book Fair	www.frankfurt-bookfair.com
Harlem Book Fair	www.qbr.com
Latino Book & Family Festival	www.latinobookfestival.com
Maui Writers Conference	www.mauiwriters.com
Shaw Guides: may be the most comprehensive listing of conferences available on the Internet.	http://writing.shawguides.com

Organizations

Association of Authors and Publishers	www.authorsandpublishers.org
Black Writers Alliance (BWA)	www.blackwriters.org
National Association of Women Writers	www.naww.org
National Writers Union	www.nwu.org
Publishers Marketing Association (PMA)	www.pma-online.org
Small Publishers, Artists, and Writers Network	www.spawn.org
Small Publishers Association of North America (SPAN): Their mission is "to advance the image and profits of independent publishers through education and marketing opportunities."	www.spannet.org
Women's National Book Association	www.wnba-books.org
The Writer's Guild	www.writersguild.org

Magazines

Black Issues Book Review	www.bibookreview.com
Foreword Magazine	www.forewordmag.com
Poets and Writers	www.pw.org
Publishers Weekly	www.publishersweekly.com
Quarterly Black Review	www.qbr.com
The Writer	www.thewritermagazine.com
Writer's Digest	www.writersdigest.com

Forms
Appendix B

Copyright
TX (Literary Works)

Copyright Office fees are subject to change. For current fees, check the Copyright Office website at www.copyright.gov, write the Copyright Office, or call (202) 707-3000.

FORM TX
For a Nondramatic Literary Work
UNITED STATES COPYRIGHT OFFICE

REGISTRATION NUMBER

TX   TXU
EFFECTIVE DATE OF REGISTRATION

Month   Day   Year

DO NOT WRITE ABOVE THIS LINE. IF YOU NEED MORE SPACE, USE A SEPARATE CONTINUATION SHEET.

1

TITLE OF THIS WORK ▼

PREVIOUS OR ALTERNATIVE TITLES ▼

PUBLICATION AS A CONTRIBUTION If this work was published as a contribution to a periodical, serial, or collection, give information about the collective work in which the contribution appeared.   Title of Collective Work ▼

If published in a periodical or serial give: Volume ▼   Number ▼   Issue Date ▼   On Pages ▼

2

a

NAME OF AUTHOR ▼

DATES OF BIRTH AND DEATH
Year Born ▼   Year Died ▼

Was this contribution to the work a "work made for hire"?
☐ Yes
☐ No

AUTHOR'S NATIONALITY OR DOMICILE
Name of Country
OR { Citizen of ▶
      Domiciled in ▶

WAS THIS AUTHOR'S CONTRIBUTION TO THE WORK
Anonymous?   ☐ Yes ☐ No
Pseudonymous?   ☐ Yes ☐ No

If the answer to either of these questions is "Yes," see detailed instructions.

NATURE OF AUTHORSHIP Briefly describe nature of material created by this author in which copyright is claimed. ▼

NOTE

Under the law, the "author" of a "work made for hire" is generally the employer, not the employee (see instructions). For any part of this work that was "made for hire" check "Yes" in the space provided, give the employer (or other person for whom the work was prepared) as "Author" of that part, and leave the space for dates of birth and death blank.

b

NAME OF AUTHOR ▼

DATES OF BIRTH AND DEATH
Year Born ▼   Year Died ▼

Was this contribution to the work a "work made for hire"?
☐ Yes
☐ No

AUTHOR'S NATIONALITY OR DOMICILE
Name of Country
OR { Citizen of ▶
      Domiciled in ▶

WAS THIS AUTHOR'S CONTRIBUTION TO THE WORK
Anonymous?   ☐ Yes ☐ No
Pseudonymous?   ☐ Yes ☐ No

If the answer to either of these questions is "Yes," see detailed instructions.

NATURE OF AUTHORSHIP Briefly describe nature of material created by this author in which copyright is claimed. ▼

c

NAME OF AUTHOR ▼

DATES OF BIRTH AND DEATH
Year Born ▼   Year Died ▼

Was this contribution to the work a "work made for hire"?
☐ Yes
☐ No

AUTHOR'S NATIONALITY OR DOMICILE
Name of Country
OR { Citizen of ▶
      Domiciled in ▶

WAS THIS AUTHOR'S CONTRIBUTION TO THE WORK
Anonymous?   ☐ Yes ☐ No
Pseudonymous?   ☐ Yes ☐ No

If the answer to either of these questions is "Yes," see detailed instructions.

NATURE OF AUTHORSHIP Briefly describe nature of material created by this author in which copyright is claimed. ▼

3

a

YEAR IN WHICH CREATION OF THIS WORK WAS COMPLETED This information must be given ◀Year in all cases.

DATE AND NATION OF FIRST PUBLICATION OF THIS PARTICULAR WORK
Complete this information Month ▶   Day ▶   Year ▶
ONLY if this work has been published.   ◀ Nation

4

See instructions before completing this space.

COPYRIGHT CLAIMANT(S) Name and address must be given even if the claimant is the same as the author given in space 2. ▼

TRANSFER If the claimant(s) named here in space 4 is (are) different from the author(s) named in space 2, give a brief statement of how the claimant(s) obtained ownership of the copyright. ▼

APPLICATION RECEIVED

ONE DEPOSIT RECEIVED

TWO DEPOSITS RECEIVED

FUNDS RECEIVED

DO NOT WRITE HERE OFFICE USE ONLY

MORE ON BACK ▶ • Complete all applicable spaces (numbers 5-9) on the reverse side of this page.
• See detailed instructions.   • Sign the form at line 8.

DO NOT WRITE HERE
Page 1 of _____ pages

EXAMINED BY	FORM TX
CHECKED BY	
☐ CORRESPONDENCE ☐ Yes	FOR COPYRIGHT OFFICE USE ONLY

DO NOT WRITE ABOVE THIS LINE. IF YOU NEED MORE SPACE, USE A SEPARATE CONTINUATION SHEET.

PREVIOUS REGISTRATION Has registration for this work, or for an earlier version of this work, already been made in the Copyright Office?

☐ Yes ☐ No If your answer is "Yes," why is another registration being sought? (Check appropriate box.) ▼

a. ☐ This is the first published edition of a work previously registered in unpublished form.

b. ☐ This is the first application submitted by this author as copyright claimant.

c. ☐ This is a changed version of the work, as shown by space 6 on this application.

If your answer is "Yes," give: **Previous Registration Number ▶**　　　**Year of Registration ▶**

5

DERIVATIVE WORK OR COMPILATION

Preexisting Material Identify any preexisting work or works that this work is based on or incorporates. ▼

a

6

Material Added to This Work Give a brief, general statement of the material that has been added to this work and in which copyright is claimed. ▼

b

See instructions before completing this space.

DEPOSIT ACCOUNT If the registration fee is to be charged to a Deposit Account established in the Copyright Office, give name and number of Account.

Name ▼　　　**Account Number ▼**

a

7

CORRESPONDENCE Give name and address to which correspondence about this application should be sent.　Name/Address/Apt/City/State/ZIP ▼

b

Area code and daytime telephone number ▶　　　Fax number ▶

Email ▶

CERTIFICATION* I, the undersigned, hereby certify that I am the

Check only one ▶

☐ author
☐ other copyright claimant
☐ owner of exclusive right(s)
☐ authorized agent of ....

Name of author or other copyright claimant, or owner of exclusive right(s) ▲

of the work identified in this application and that the statements made by me in this application are correct to the best of my knowledge.

8

Typed or printed name and date ▼ If this application gives a date of publication in space 3, do not sign and submit it before that date.

....　**Date ▶** ....

Handwritten signature (X) ▼

X _____

Certificate will be mailed in window envelope to this address:

Name ▼

Number/Street/Apt ▼

City/State/ZIP ▼

YOU MUST:
• Complete all necessary spaces
• Sign your application in space 8

SEND ALL 3 ELEMENTS IN THE SAME PACKAGE:
1. Application form
2. Nonrefundable filing fee in check or money order payable to *Register of Copyrights*
3. Deposit material

MAIL TO:
Library of Congress
Copyright Office
101 Independence Avenue, S.E.
Washington, D.C. 20559-6000

Fees are subject to change. For current fees, check the Copyright Office website at www.copyright.gov, write the Copyright Office, or call (202) 707-3000.

9

*17 U.S.C. § 506(e): Any person who knowingly makes a false representation of a material fact in the application for copyright registration provided for by section 409, or in any written statement filed in connection with the application, shall be fined not more than $2,500.

Rev: June 2002—20,000 Web Rev: June 2002 ♻ Printed on recycled paper　　　U.S. Government Printing Office: 2000-461-113/20.021

Copyright

TX Short Form

Instructions for Short Form TX

For nondramatic literary works, including fiction and nonfiction, books, short stories, poems, collections of poetry, essays, articles in serials, and computer programs

USE THIS FORM IF—

1. You are the **only** author and copyright owner of this work, *and*
2. The work was **not** made for hire, *and*
3. The work is completely new (does not contain a substantial amount of material that has been previously published or registered or is in the public domain).

If any of the above does not apply, you must use standard Form TX.
NOTE: *Short Form TX is not appropriate for an anonymous author who does not wish to reveal his or her identity.*

HOW TO COMPLETE SHORT FORM TX

- Type or print in black ink.
- Be clear and legible. (Your certificate of registration will be copied from your form.)
- Give only the information requested.

NOTE: You may use a continuation sheet (Form __/CON) to list individual titles in a collection. Complete Space A and list the individual titles under Space C on the back page. Space B is not applicable to short forms.

1 Title of This Work

You must give a title. If there is no title, state "UNTITLED." If you are registering an unpublished collection, give the collection title you want to appear in our records (for example: "Joan's Poems, Volume 1"). Alternative title: If the work is known by two titles, you also may give the second title. If the work has been published as part of a larger work (including a periodical), give the title of that larger work in addition to the title of the contribution.

2 Name and Address of Author and Owner of the Copyright

Give your name and mailing address. You may include your pseudonym (followed by "pseud." Also, give the nation of which you are a citizen or where you have your domicile (i.e., permanent residence). Please give daytime phone and fax numbers and email address, if available.

3 Year of Creation

Give the latest year in which you completed the work you are registering at this time. A work is "created" when it is written down, stored in a computer, or otherwise "fixed" in a tangible form.

4 Publication

If the work has been published (i.e., if copies have been distributed to the public), give the complete date of publication (month, day, and year) and the nation where the publication first took place.

5 Type of Authorship in This Work

Check the box or boxes that describe your authorship in the copy you are sending with the application. For example, if you are

registering a story and are planning to add illustrations later, check only the box for "text."

A "compilation" of terms of data is a selection, coordination, or arrangement of such information into a chart, directory, or other form. A compilation of previously published or public domain material must be registered using a standard Form TX.

6 Signature of Author

Sign the application in black ink and check the appropriate box. The person signing the application should be the author or his/her authorized agent.

7 Person to Contact for Rights and Permissions

This space is optional. You may give the name and address of the person or organization to contact for permission to use the work. You may also provide phone, fax, or email information.

8 Certificate Will Be Mailed

This space must be completed. Your certificate of registration will be mailed in a window envelope to this address. Also, if the Copyright Office needs to contact you, we will write to this address.

9 Deposit Account

Complete this space only if you currently maintain a deposit account in the Copyright Office.

MAIL WITH THE FORM

A $30 filing fee in the form of a check or money order (*no cash*) payable to "Register of Copyrights,"
and
- One or two copies of the work. If the work is unpublished, send one copy. If published, send two copies of the best published edition. (If first published outside the U.S., send one copy either as first published or of the best edition.) **Note:** Inquire about special requirements for works first published before 1978. Copies submitted become the property of the U.S. Government.

Mail everything (**application form, copy or copies, and fee**) *in one package* to:

Library of Congress
Copyright Office
101 Independence Avenue, S.E.
Washington, D.C. 20559-6000

QUESTIONS? Call (202) 707-3000 [TTY: (202) 707-6737] between 8:30 a.m. and 5:00 p.m. eastern time, Monday through Friday. For forms and informational circulars, call (202) 707-9100 24 hours a day, 7 days a week, or download them from the Copyright Office website at *www.copyright.gov*. Selected informational circulars but not forms are available from Fax-on-Demand at (202) 707-2600.

Copyright Office fees are subject to change.
For current fees, check the Copyright Office
website at *www.copyright.gov*, write the Copyright Office, or call (202) 707-3000.

SHORT FORM TX
For a Nondramatic Literary Work

UNITED STATES COPYRIGHT OFFICE
Registration Number

TX   TXU

Effective Date of Registration

Application Received

Examined By

Deposit Received
One   Two

Correspondence

Fee Received

TYPE OR PRINT IN BLACK INK. DO NOT WRITE ABOVE THIS LINE.

Title of This Work: | **1** |

Alternative title or title of
larger work in which this
work was published:

**Name and Address of
Author and Owner of the
Copyright:** | **2** |

Nationality or domicile:
Phone, fax, and email: | Phone (   )   Fax (   )
Email

Year of Creation: | **3** |

**If work has been published,
Date and Nation of
Publication:** | **4** | a. Date _____ *(Month, day, and year all required)*
                                Month   Day   Year
b. Nation

**Type of Authorship
in This Work:** | **5** | ❏ Text (includes fiction, nonfiction, poetry, computer programs, etc.)
❏ Illustrations
❏ Photographs
Check all that this author created. | ❏ Compilation of terms or data

Signature: | **6** | *I certify that the statements made by me in this application are correct to the best of my knowledge.* Check one:
❏ Author ❏ Authorized agent

Registration cannot be
completed without a
signature. | X _

OPTIONAL

**Name and Address of
Person to Contact for
Rights and Permissions:**
Phone, fax, and email: | **7** | ❏ Check here if same as #2 above.

Phone (   )   Fax (   )
Email

8 | Name ▼ | **9** | Deposit Account # _____
Name _____

Certificate
will be
mailed in
window
envelope to
this address: | Number/Street/Apt ▼ |

City/State/ZIP ▼

Complete this space only
if you currently hold a
Deposit Account in
the Copyright
Office.

DO NOT WRITE HERE   Page 1 of ____ pages

*17 U.S.C. § 506(e): Any person who knowingly makes a false representation of a material fact in the application for copyright registration provided for by section 409, or in any written statement filed in connection with the application, shall be fined not more than $2,500.

Rev: June 2002—20,000   Web Rev: June 2002   ♻ Printed on recycled paper

U.S. Government Printing Office: 2000-461-113/20,021

117

Copyright
PA (Performing Arts)

118

FORM PA
For a Work of the Performing Arts
UNITED STATES COPYRIGHT OFFICE

REGISTRATION NUMBER

PA   PAU

EFFECTIVE DATE OF REGISTRATION

Month   Day   Year

DO NOT WRITE ABOVE THIS LINE. IF YOU NEED MORE SPACE, USE A SEPARATE CONTINUATION SHEET.

1 TITLE OF THIS WORK ▼

PREVIOUS OR ALTERNATIVE TITLES ▼

NATURE OF THIS WORK ▼ See instructions

2

a NAME OF AUTHOR ▼

DATES OF BIRTH AND DEATH
Year Born ▼   Year Died ▼

Was this contribution to the work a "work made for hire"?
☐ Yes
☐ No

AUTHOR'S NATIONALITY OR DOMICILE
Name of Country
OR { Citizen of ....
Domiciled in ....

WAS THIS AUTHOR'S CONTRIBUTION TO THE WORK
Anonymous?   ☐ Yes ☐ No
Pseudonymous?   ☐ Yes ☐ No

If the answer to either of these questions is "Yes," see detailed instructions.

NATURE OF AUTHORSHIP Briefly describe nature of material created by this author in which copyright is claimed. ▼

NOTE

Under the law, the "author" of a "work made for hire" is generally the employer, not the employee (see instructions). For any part of this work that was "made for hire" check "Yes" in the space provided, give the employer (or other person for whom the work was prepared) as "Author" of that part, and leave the space for dates of birth and death blank.

b NAME OF AUTHOR ▼

DATES OF BIRTH AND DEATH
Year Born ▼   Year Died ▼

Was this contribution to the work a "work made for hire"?
☐ Yes
☐ No

AUTHOR'S NATIONALITY OR DOMICILE
Name of Country
OR { Citizen of ....
Domiciled in ....

WAS THIS AUTHOR'S CONTRIBUTION TO THE WORK
Anonymous?   ☐ Yes ☐ No
Pseudonymous?   ☐ Yes ☐ No

If the answer to either of these questions is "Yes," see detailed instructions.

NATURE OF AUTHORSHIP Briefly describe nature of material created by this author in which copyright is claimed. ▼

c NAME OF AUTHOR ▼

DATES OF BIRTH AND DEATH
Year Born ▼   Year Died ▼

Was this contribution to the work a "work made for hire"?
☐ Yes
☐ No

AUTHOR'S NATIONALITY OR DOMICILE
Name of Country
OR { Citizen of ....
Domiciled in ....

WAS THIS AUTHOR'S CONTRIBUTION TO THE WORK
Anonymous?   ☐ Yes ☐ No
Pseudonymous?   ☐ Yes ☐ No

If the answer to either of these questions is "Yes," see detailed instructions.

NATURE OF AUTHORSHIP Briefly describe nature of material created by this author in which copyright is claimed. ▼

3

a YEAR IN WHICH CREATION OF THIS WORK WAS COMPLETED   This information must be given   Year   in all cases.

b DATE AND NATION OF FIRST PUBLICATION OF THIS PARTICULAR WORK
Complete this information   Month ....   Day ....   Year ....
ONLY if this work has been published.   Nation

4

See instructions before completing this space.

COPYRIGHT CLAIMANT(S) Name and address must be given even if the claimant is the same as the author given in space 2. ▼

TRANSFER If the claimant(s) named here in space 4 is (are) different from the author(s) named in space 2, give a brief statement of how the claimant(s) obtained ownership of the copyright. ▼

APPLICATION RECEIVED
ONE DEPOSIT RECEIVED
TWO DEPOSITS RECEIVED
FUNDS RECEIVED

DO NOT WRITE HERE OFFICE USE ONLY

MORE ON BACK ▶ • Complete all applicable spaces (numbers 5-9) on the reverse side of this page.
• See detailed instructions.   • Sign the form at line 8.

DO NOT WRITE HERE
Page 1 of .... pages

EXAMINED BY	FORM PA
CHECKED BY	
☐ CORRESPONDENCE ☐ Yes	FOR COPYRIGHT OFFICE USE ONLY

DO NOT WRITE ABOVE THIS LINE. IF YOU NEED MORE SPACE, USE A SEPARATE CONTINUATION SHEET.

PREVIOUS REGISTRATION Has registration for this work, or for an earlier version of this work, already been made in the Copyright Office?
☐ Yes ☐ No If your answer is "Yes," why is another registration being sought? (Check appropriate box.) ▼ If your answer is No, do not check box A, B, or C.
a. ☐ This is the first published edition of a work previously registered in unpublished form.
b. ☐ This is the first application submitted by this author as copyright claimant.
c. ☐ This is a changed version of the work, as shown by space 6 on this application.
If your answer is "Yes," give: **Previous Registration Number ▼**   **Year of Registration ▼**

5

DERIVATIVE WORK OR COMPILATION Complete both space 6a and 6b for a derivative work; complete only 6b for a compilation.
Preexisting Material Identify any preexisting work or works that this work is based on or incorporates. ▼

a

6

See instructions
before completing
this space.

Material Added to This Work Give a brief, general statement of the material that has been added to this work and in which copyright is claimed. ▼

b

DEPOSIT ACCOUNT If the registration fee is to be charged to a Deposit Account established in the Copyright Office, give name and number of Account.
Name ▼   **Account Number ▼**

a

7

CORRESPONDENCE Give name and address to which correspondence about this application should be sent. Name/Address/Apt/City/State/ZIP ▼

b

Area code and daytime telephone number   (   )   Fax number   (   )
Email

CERTIFICATION* I, the undersigned, hereby certify that I am the
Check only one ▶
☐ author
☐ other copyright claimant
☐ owner of exclusive right(s)
☐ authorized agent of
Name of author or other copyright claimant, or owner of exclusive right(s) ▲
of the work identified in this application and that the statements made by me in this application are correct to the best of my knowledge.

8

Typed or printed name and date ▼ If this application gives a date of publication in space 3, do not sign and submit it before that date.

Date

Handwritten signature (X) ▼
X

Certificate will be mailed in window envelope to this address:	Name ▼
	Number/Street/Apt ▼
	City/State/ZIP ▼

YOU MUST:
• Complete all necessary spaces
• Sign your application in space 8
SEND ALL 3 ELEMENTS IN THE SAME PACKAGE:
1. Application form
2. Nonrefundable filing fee in check or money order payable to *Register of Copyrights*
3. Deposit material
MAIL TO:
Library of Congress
Copyright Office
101 Independence Avenue, S.E.
Washington, D.C. 20559-6000

Fees are subject to change. For current fees, check the Copyright Office website at www.copyright.gov, write the Copyright Office, or call (202) 707-3000.

9

*17 U.S.C. § 506(e): Any person who knowingly makes a false representation of a material fact in the application for copyright registration provided for by section 409, or in any written statement filed in connection with the application, shall be fined not more than $2,500.

Rev. June 2002—20,000   Web Rev: June 2002   ♻ Printed on recycled paper

U.S. Government Printing Office: 2000-461-113/20.021

Copyright

PA Short Form

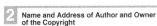

✍ Instructions for Short Form PA ✍

For works in the performing arts (except audiovisual works)

USE THIS FORM IF—

1. You are the **only** author and copyright owner of this work, *and*
2. The work was **not** made for hire, *and*
3. The work is completely new (does not contain a substantial amount of material that has been previously published or registered or is in the public domain) and is not an audiovisual work.

If any of the above does not apply, you must use standard Form PA.

NOTE: *Short Form PA is not appropriate for an anonymous author who does not wish to reveal his or her identity and may not be used for audiovisual works, including motion pictures.*

HOW TO COMPLETE SHORT FORM PA

Type or print in black ink.

• Be clear and legible. (Your certificate of registration will be copied from your form.)

• Give only the information requested.

NOTE: You may use a continuation sheet (Form __/CON) to list individual titles in a collection. Complete Space A and list the individual titles under Space C on the back page. Space B is not applicable to short forms.

---

1 **Title of This Work**

You must give a title. If there is no title, state "UNTITLED." Alternative title: If the work is known by two titles, you also may give the second title. Or if the work has been published as part of a larger work, give the title of that larger work, in addition to the title of the contribution.

If you are registering an unpublished collection, give the collection title you want to appear in our records (for example: "Songs by Alice, Volume 1"). Be sure to keep a personal record of the songs you have included in the collection. If you want the certificate of registration to list the individual titles as well as the collection title, use a continuation sheet (Form___/CON).

2 **Name and Address of Author and Owner of the Copyright**

Give your name and mailing address. You may include your pseudonym followed by "pseud." Also, give the nation of which you are a citizen or where you have your domicile (i.e., permanent residence). Please give daytime phone and fax numbers and email address, if available.

3 **Year of Creation**

Give the latest year in which you completed the work you are registering at this time. A work is "created" when it is written down, recorded, or otherwise "fixed" in a tangible form.

4 **Publication**

If the work has been published (i.e., if copies have been distributed to the public), give the complete date of publication (month, day, and year) and the nation where the publication first took place.

5 **Type of Authorship in This Work**

Check the box or boxes that describe the kind of material you are registering. Check *only* the authorship included in the copy, tape, or CD you are sending with the application. For example, if you are registering lyrics and plan to add music later, check only the box for "lyrics."

6 **Signature of Author**

Sign the application in black ink and check the appropriate box. The person signing the application should be the author or his/her authorized agent.

7 **Person to Contact for Rights and Permissions**

This space is optional. You may give the name and address of the person or organization to contact for permission to use the work. You may also provide phone, fax, or email information.

8 **Certificate Will Be Mailed**

This space must be completed. Your certificate of registration will be mailed in a window envelope to this address. Also, if the Copyright Office needs to contact you, we will write to this address.

9 **Deposit Account**

Complete this space only if you currently maintain a deposit account in the Copyright Office.

MAIL WITH THE FORM—
• A $30 filing fee in the form of a check or money order (*no cash*) payable to "Register of Copyrights," **and**
• One or two copies of the work. If the work is unpublished, send one copy, tape, or CD. If published, send two copies of the best published edition if the work is in printed form, such as sheet music, or one copy of the best published edition if the work is recorded on a tape or disk.
Note: Inquire about special requirements for works first published outside the United States or before 1978. Copies submitted become the property of the U.S. Government.
Mail everything (**application form, copy or copies, and fee**) *in one package* to: Library of Congress, Copyright Office
101 Independence Avenue, S.E.
Washington, D.C. 20559-6000

QUESTIONS? Call (202) 707-3000 [TTY: (202) 707-6737] between 8:30 a.m. and 5:00 p.m. eastern time, Monday through Friday except federal holidays. For forms and informational circulars, call (202) 707-9100 24 hours a day, 7 days a week, or download them from the Internet at *www.copyright.gov*. Selected informational circulars but not forms are available from Fax-on-Demand at (202) 707-2600.

PRIVACY ACT ADVISORY STATEMENT **Required by the Privacy Act of 1974 (P.L. 93-579)**
The authority for requesting this information is title 17 U.S.C., secs. 409 and 410. Furnishing the requested information is voluntary. But if the information is not furnished, it may be necessary to delay or refuse registration and you may not be entitled to certain relief, remedies, and benefits provided in chapters 4 and 5 of title 17 U.S.C.
The principal uses of the requested information are the establishment and maintenance of a public record and the examination of the application for compliance with the registration requirements of the copyright law.
Other routine uses include public inspection and copying, preparation of public indexes, preparation of public catalogs of copyright registrations, and preparation of search reports upon request.
NOTE: No other advisory statement will be given in connection with this application. Please keep this statement and refer to it if we communicate with you regarding this application.

Copyright Office fees are subject to change.
For current fees, check the Copyright Office
website at www.copyright.gov, write the Copyright Office, or call (202) 707-3000.

Short Form PA
For a Work of the Performing Arts
UNITED STATES COPYRIGHT OFFICE

Registration Number

PA   PAU
Effective Date of Registration

Examined By

Application Received

Deposit Received
One | Two

Correspondence ☐
Fee Received

TYPE OR PRINT IN BLACK INK. DO NOT WRITE ABOVE THIS LINE.

1 Title of This Work:

Alternative title or title of
larger work in which this
work was published:

2 Name and Address of
Author and Owner of the
Copyright:

Nationality or domicile:
Phone, fax, and email:

Phone ( )   Fax ( )
Email:

3 Year of Creation:

4 If work has been published,
Date and Nation of
Publication:

a. Date _____
Month   Day   Year   (Month, day, and
year all required)
b. Nation

5 Type of Authorship
in This Work:
Check all that this author created.

☐ Music   ☐ Other text (includes dramas, screenplays, etc.)
☐ Lyrics   (If your work is a motion picture or other audiovisual work, use the Standard Form PA.)

6 Signature:
(Registration cannot be completed
without a signature.)

I certify that the statements made by me in this application are correct to the best of my knowledge.* Check one:
☐ Author
☐ Authorized agent   X_ _

7 Name and Address of
Person to Contact for
Rights and Permissions:

OPTIONAL

☐ Check here if same as #2 above.

Phone, fax, and email:

Phone ( )   Fax ( )
Email:

8
Certificate
will be
mailed in
window
envelope to
this address:

Name ▼

Number/Street/Apt ▼

City/State/ZIP ▼

9 Deposit Account #_____
Name _____

Complete this space only
if you currently hold a
Deposit Account in
the Copyright
Office.

DO NOT WRITE HERE   Page 1 of ____ pages

*17 U.S.C. § 506(e): Any person who knowingly makes a false representation of a material fact in the application for copyright registration provided for by section 409, or in any written statement filed in connection with
the application, shall be fined not more than $2,500.

Rev: June 2002—20,000   Web Rev: June 2002   ♻ Printed on recycled paper

U.S. Government Printing Office: 2000-461-113/20,021

Copyright
SE (Serial Works)

FORM SE
For a Serial
UNITED STATES COPYRIGHT OFFICE

REGISTRATION NUMBER

U

EFFECTIVE DATE OF REGISTRATION

Month   Day   Year

DO NOT WRITE ABOVE THIS LINE. IF YOU NEED MORE SPACE, USE A SEPARATE CONTINUATION SHEET.

1 TITLE OF THIS SERIAL ▼

Volume ▼   Number ▼   Date on Copies ▼   Frequency of Publication ▼

PREVIOUS OR ALTERNATIVE TITLES ▼

2 a NAME OF AUTHOR ▼   DATES OF BIRTH AND DEATH
Year Born ▼   Year Died ▼

Was this contribution to the work a "work made for hire"?   AUTHOR'S NATIONALITY OR DOMICILE   Name of Country
☐ Yes   OR { Citizen of ▶ _____
☐ No   Domiciled in ▶ _____

WAS THIS AUTHOR'S CONTRIBUTION TO THE WORK
Anonymous?   ☐ Yes ☐ No   If the answer to either of these questions is "Yes," see detailed instructions.
Pseudonymous?   ☐ Yes ☐ No

NATURE OF AUTHORSHIP   Briefly describe nature of material created by this author in which copyright is claimed. ▼
☐ Collective Work   Other:

NOTE
Under the law, the "author" of a "work made for hire" is generally the employer, not the employee (see instructions). For any part of this work that was "made for hire" check "Yes" in the space provided, give the employer (or other person for whom the work was prepared) as "Author" of that part, and leave the space for dates of birth and death blank.

b NAME OF AUTHOR ▼   DATES OF BIRTH AND DEATH
Year Born ▼   Year Died ▼

Was this contribution to the work a "work made for hire"?   AUTHOR'S NATIONALITY OR DOMICILE   Name of Country
☐ Yes   OR { Citizen of ▶ _____
☐ No   Domiciled in ▶ _____

WAS THIS AUTHOR'S CONTRIBUTION TO THE WORK
Anonymous?   ☐ Yes ☐ No   If the answer to either of these questions is "Yes," see detailed instructions.
Pseudonymous?   ☐ Yes ☐ No

NATURE OF AUTHORSHIP   Briefly describe nature of material created by this author in which copyright is claimed. ▼
☐ Collective Work   Other:

c NAME OF AUTHOR ▼   DATES OF BIRTH AND DEATH
Year Born ▼   Year Died ▼

Was this contribution to the work a "work made for hire"?   AUTHOR'S NATIONALITY OR DOMICILE   Name of Country
☐ Yes   OR { Citizen of ▶ _____
☐ No   Domiciled in ▶ _____

WAS THIS AUTHOR'S CONTRIBUTION TO THE WORK
Anonymous?   ☐ Yes ☐ No   If the answer to either of these questions is "Yes," see detailed instructions.
Pseudonymous?   ☐ Yes ☐ No

NATURE OF AUTHORSHIP   Briefly describe nature of material created by this author in which copyright is claimed. ▼
☐ Collective Work   Other:

3 a YEAR IN WHICH CREATION OF THIS ISSUE WAS COMPLETED   This information must be given ◀ Year in all cases.
b DATE AND NATION OF FIRST PUBLICATION OF THIS PARTICULAR ISSUE
Complete this information ONLY if this work has been published.   Month ▶ _____ Day ▶ _____ Year ▶ _____ ◀ Nation

4 COPYRIGHT CLAIMANT(S) Name and address must be given even if the claimant is the same as the author given in space 2. ▼

See instructions before completing this space.

TRANSFER If the claimant(s) named here in space 4 is (are) different from the author(s) named in space 2, give a brief statement of how the claimant(s) obtained ownership of the copyright. ▼

DO NOT WRITE HERE   OFFICE USE ONLY
APPLICATION RECEIVED
ONE DEPOSIT RECEIVED
TWO DEPOSITS RECEIVED
REMITTANCE NUMBER AND DATE

MORE ON BACK ▶   • Complete all applicable spaces (numbers 5-11) on the reverse side of this page.
• See detailed instructions.   • Sign the form at line 10.

DO NOT WRITE HERE
Page 1 of _____ pages

122

EXAMINED BY	FORM SE
CHECKED BY	
☐ CORRESPONDENCE Yes	FOR COPYRIGHT OFFICE USE ONLY

DO NOT WRITE ABOVE THIS LINE. IF YOU NEED MORE SPACE, USE A SEPARATE CONTINUATION SHEET.

PREVIOUS REGISTRATION Has registration for this work, or for an earlier version of this work, already been made in the Copyright Office? **5**
☐ Yes ☐ No If your answer is "Yes," why is another registration being sought? (Check appropriate box.) ▼
a. ☐ This is the first published edition of a work previously registered in unpublished form.
b. ☐ This is the first application submitted by this author as copyright claimant.
c. ☐ This is a changed version of the work, as shown by space 6 on this application.
If your answer is "Yes," give: **Previous Registration Number** ▼   **Year of Registration** ▼

DERIVATIVE WORK OR COMPILATION Complete both space 6a and 6b for a derivative work; complete only 6b for a compilation. **6**
Preexisting Material Identify any preexisting work or works that this work is based on or incorporates. ▼   **a**
See instructions before completing this space.
Material Added to This Work Give a brief, general statement of the material that has been added to this work and in which copyright is claimed. ▼   **b**

DEPOSIT ACCOUNT If the registration fee is to be charged to a Deposit Account established in the Copyright Office, give name and number of Account. **7**
Name ▼   **Account Number** ▼   **a**

CORRESPONDENCE Give name and address to which correspondence about this application should be sent.   Name / Address / Apt / City / State / ZIP ▼   **b**

Area code and daytime telephone number ▶   Fax number   ▶
Email ▶

CERTIFICATION* I, the undersigned, hereby certify that I am the **8**
Check only one ▶
☐ author
☐ other copyright claimant
☐ owner of exclusive right(s)
☐ authorized agent of _____
of the work identified in this application and that the statements made by me in this application are correct to the best of my knowledge.
Name of author or other copyright claimant, or owner of exclusive right(s) ▲

Typed or printed name and date ▼ If this application gives a date of publication in space 3, do not sign and submit it before that date.
_____ Date ▶ _____

Handwritten signature (X) ▼
X _____

Certificate will be mailed in window envelope to this address:	Name ▼	**9** YOU MUST: • Complete all necessary spaces • Sign your application in space 8
	Number/Street/Apt ▼	SEND ALL 3 ELEMENTS IN THE SAME PACKAGE: 1. Application form 2. Nonrefundable filing fee in check or money order payable to Register of Copyrights 3. Deposit material
	City/State/ZIP ▼	MAIL TO: Library of Congress Copyright Office 101 Independence Avenue, S.E. Washington, D.C. 20559-6000

Fees are subject to change. For current fees, check the Copyright Office website at www.copyright.gov, write the Copyright Office, or call (202) 707-3000.

*17 U.S.C. § 506(e): Any person who knowingly makes a false representation of a material fact in the application for copyright registration provided for by section 409, or in any written statement filed in connection with the application, shall be fined not more than $2,500.

Rev: June 2002—20,000 Web Rev: June 2002 ♻ Printed on recycled paper   U.S. Government Printing Office: 2000-461-113/20,021

Copyright
SE/Group

✐ Form SE/Group ✐

Read these instructions before completing this form.
Make sure all applicable spaces have been filled in before you return this form.

BASIC INFORMATION

When to Use this Form: All the following conditions must be met in order to use this form. If any one of the conditions does not apply, you must register the issues separately using Form SE or Short Form SE.
1. You must have given a complimentary subscription for two copies of the serial to the Library of Congress, confirmed by letter to:
   Library of Congress
   Group Periodicals Registration
   Washington, D.C. 20540-4161
   Subscription copies must be mailed separately to the same address.
2. The claim must be in the collective works.
3. The works must be essentially all new collective works or issues.
4. Each issue must be a work made for hire.
5. The author(s) and claimant(s) must be the same person(s) or organization(s) for all the issues.
6. Each issue must have been created no more than 1 year prior to publication.
7. All issues in the group must have been published within the same calendar year.
   For copyright purposes, serials are defined as works issued or intended to be issued in successive parts bearing numerical or chronological designations and intended to be continued indefinitely. The classification "serial" includes periodicals, newspapers, magazines, bulletins, newsletters, annuals, journals, proceedings of societies, and other similar works.

Which Issues May Be Included in a Group Registration: You may register two or more issues of a serial published at inter-vals of 1 week or longer under the same continuing title, provided that the issues were published within a 90-day period during the same calendar year.

Deposit to Accompany Application: Send one copy of each issue included in the group registration with the application and fee.

Fee: A nonrefundable filing fee of $15 (minimum fee: $45) FOR EACH ISSUE LISTED ON FORM SE/GROUP must be sent with the application or charged to an active deposit account in the Copyright Office. Make checks payable to **Register of Copyrights. Fees are effective July 1, 2002.**

Mailing Instructions: Send the application, deposit copies, and fee together in the same package to: *Library of Congress, Copyright Office, 101 Independence Ave., S.E., Washington, D.C. 20559-6000.*

International Standard Serial Number (ISSN): ISSN is an internationally accepted code to identify serial publications. If a published serial has not been assigned an ISSN, application forms and additional information my be obtained from Library of Congress, National Serials Data Program, Serial Record Division, Washington, D.C. 20540-4160. Call (202) 707-6452. Or obtain information via the Internet at *www.loc.gov/issn.* Do not contact the Copyright Office for ISSNs.

Collective Work: The term "collective work" refers to a work, such as a serial issue, in which a number of contributions are assembled into a collective whole. A claim in the "collective work" extends to all copyrightable authorship created by employees of the author, as well as any independent contributions in which the claimant has acquired ownership of the copyright.

Publication: The statute defines "publication" as "the distribution of copies or phonorecords of a work to the public by sale or other transfer of ownership, or by rental, lease, or lending." A work is also "published" if there has been an "offering to distribute copies or phonorecords to a group of persons for purposes of further distribution, public performance, or public display."

Creation: A work is "created" when it is fixed in a copy (or phonorecord) for the first time. For a serial, the year in which the collective work was completed is the creation date.

Work Made for Hire: A "work made for hire" is defined as: (1) a work prepared by an employee within the scope of his or her employment; or (2) a work specially ordered or commissioned for certain uses (including use as a contribution to a collective work), if the parties expressly agree in a written instrument signed by them that the work shall be considered a work made for hire. The employer is the author of a work made for hire.

The Copyright Notice: Before March 1, 1989, the use of copyright notice was mandatory on all published works, and any work first published before that date should have carried a notice. For works first published on and after March 1, 1989, use of the copyright notice is optional. For more information about copyright notice, see Circular 3, "Copyright Notice."

For Further Information: To speak to an information specialist, call (202) 707-3000 (TTY: (202) 707-6737). Recorded information is available 24 hours a day. Order forms and other publications from the address at the bottom of page 2, or call the Forms and Publications Hotline at (202) 707-9100. Circulars (but not forms) are available via fax. Call (202) 707-2600 from a touchtone phone. Access and download circulars, forms, and other information from the Copyright Office website at *www.copyright.gov.*

LINE-BY-LINE INSTRUCTIONS

1 SPACE 1: Title and Date of Publication

Give the complete title of the serial, followed by the International Standard Serial Number (ISSN), if available. List the issues in the order of publication. For each issue, give the volume, number, and issue date appearing on the copies, followed by the complete date of publication, including month, day, and year. If you have not previously registered this identical title under Section 408 of the Copyright Act, please indicate by checking the box.

2 SPACE 2: Author and Copyright Claimant

Give the fullest form of the author and claimant's name and mailing address. If there are joint authors and claimants, give the names and addresses of all the author/claimants. If the work is not of U.S. origin, add the citizenship or domicile of the author/claimant, or the nation of publication.

Certification: The application cannot be accepted unless it bears the handwritten signature of the copyright claimant or the duly authorized agent of the copyright claimant.

Person to Contact for Correspondence about this Claim: Give the name, address, telephone number, area code, fax number, and email address (if available) of the person to whom any correspondence concerning this claim should be addressed. Give the address only if it is different from the address for mailing of the certificate.

Deposit Account: If the filing fee is to be charged against a deposit account in the Copyright Office, give the name and number of the account in this space. Otherwise, leave the space blank and forward the filing fee with your application and deposit.

Mailing Address of Certificate: This address must be complete and legible since the certificate will be mailed in a window envelope.
(Information continues on reverse)

Copyright Office fees are subject to change.
For current fees, check the Copyright Office
website at www.copyright.gov, write the Copyright Office, or call (202) 707-3000.

FORM SE/Group
UNITED STATES COPYRIGHT OFFICE

REGISTRATION NUMBER

EFFECTIVE DATE OF REGISTRATION

APPLICATION RECEIVED

ONE DEPOSIT RECEIVED

EXAMINED BY   CORRESPONDENCE ☐

DO NOT WRITE ABOVE THIS LINE.

1

List in order of publication

No previous registration under identical title ☐

TITLE ▼   ISSN▼

	Volume▼	Number▼	Issue date on copies▼	Month, day, and year of publication ▼
1.				
2.				
3.				
4.				
5.				
6.				
7.				
8.				
9.				
10.				
11.				
12.				
13.				
14.				

2 NAME AND ADDRESS OF THE AUTHOR/COPYRIGHT CLAIMANT IN THESE COLLECTIVE WORKS MADE FOR HIRE ▼

FOR NON-U.S. WORKS: Author's citizenship ▼   Domicile ▼   Nation of publication ▼

CERTIFICATION*: I, the undersigned, hereby certify that I am the copyright claimant or the authorized agent of the copyright claimant of the works identified in this application, that all the conditions specified in the instructions on the back of this form are met, that I have deposited two complimentary subscription copies with the Library of Congress, and that the statements made by me in this application are correct to the best of my knowledge.

Handwritten signature (X) _____

Typed or printed name _____

PERSON TO CONTACT FOR CORRESPONDENCE ABOUT THIS CLAIM
Name _____   Daytime telephone _____
Address (if other than given below) _____

Fax _____   Email _____

Certificate will be mailed in window envelope to this address:

Name▼ _____
Number/Street/Apt ▼ _____
City/State/ZIP▼ _____

DEPOSIT ACCOUNT
Account number _____
Name of account _____

MAIL TO:
Library of Congress
Copyright Office
101 Independence Avenue, S.E.
Washington, D.C. 20559-6000

*17 U.S.C. §506(e): Any person who knowingly makes a false representation of a material fact in the application for copyright registration provided for by section 409, or in any written statement filed in connection with the application, shall be fined not more than $2,500.

Rev: June 2002—20,000 Web Rev: June 2002 ♻ Printed on recycled paper

U.S. Government Printing Office: 2000-461-113/20,021

125

Copyright
SR (Sound Recordings)

☺ Form SR ☺

Detach and read these instructions before completing this form.
Make sure all applicable spaces have been filled in before you return this form.

BASIC INFORMATION

When to Use This Form: Use Form SR for registration of published or unpublished sound recordings. It should be used when the copyright claim is limited to the sound recording itself, and it may also be used where the same copyright claimant is seeking simultaneous registration of the underlying musical, dramatic, or literary work embodied in the phonorecord.

With one exception, "sound recordings" are works that result from the fixation of a series of musical, spoken, or other sounds. The exception is for the audio portions of audiovisual works, such as a motion picture soundtrack or an audio cassette accompanying a filmstrip. These are considered a part of the audiovisual work as a whole.

Deposit to Accompany Application: An application for copyright registration must be accompanied by a deposit consisting of phonorecords representing the entire work for which registration is to be made.

Unpublished Work: Deposit one complete phonorecord.

Published Work: Deposit two complete phonorecords of the best edition, together with "any printed or other visually perceptible material" published with the phonorecords.

Work First Published Outside the United States: Deposit one complete phonorecord of the first foreign edition.

Contribution to a Collective Work: Deposit one complete phonorecord of the best edition of the collective work.

The Copyright Notice: Before March 1, 1989, the use of copyright notice was mandatory on all published works, and any work first published before that date should have carried a notice. For works first published on and after March 1, 1989, use of the copyright notice is optional. For more information about copyright notice, see Circular 3, "Copyright Notices."

For Further Information: To speak to an information specialist, call (202) 707-3000 (TTY: (202) 707-6737). Recorded information is available 24 hours a day. Order forms and other publications from Library of Congress, Copyright Office, 101 Independence Avenue, S.E., Washington, D.C. 20559-6000 or call the Forms and Publications Hotline at (202) 707-9100. Most circulars (but not forms) are available via fax. Call (202) 707-2600 from a touchtone phone. Access and download circulars, forms, and other information from the Copyright Office Website at *www.copyright.gov.*

LINE-BY-LINE INSTRUCTIONS

Please type or print neatly using black ink. The form is used to produce the certificate.

1 SPACE 1: Title

Title of This Work: Every work submitted for copyright registration must be given a title that particular work. If the phonorecords or any accompanying printed material bears a title (or an identifying phrase that could serve as a title), transcribe that wording completely and exactly on the application. Indexing of the registration and future identification of the work may depend on the information you give here.

Previous, Alternative, or Contents Titles: Complete this space if there are any previous or alternative titles for the work under which someone searching for the registration might be likely to look, or under which a document pertaining to the work might be recorded. You may also give the individual contents titles, if any, in this space or you may use a Continuation Sheet. Circle the term that describes the titles given.

2 SPACE 2: Author(s)

General Instructions: After reading these instructions, decide who are the "authors" of this work for copyright purposes. Then, unless the work is a "collective work," give the requested information about every "author" who contributed any appreciable amount of copyrightable matter to this version of the work. If you need further space, request additional Continuation Sheets. In the case of a collective work such as a collection of previously published or registered sound recordings, give information about the author of the collective work as a whole. If you are submitting this Form SR to cover the recorded musical, dramatic, or literary work as well as the sound recording itself, it is important for space 2 to include full information about the various authors of all of the material covered by the copyright claim, making clear the nature of each author's contribution.

Name of Author: The fullest form of the author's name should be given. Unless the work was "made for hire," the individual who actually created the work is its "author." In the case of a work made for hire, the statute provides that "the employer or other person for whom the work was prepared is considered the author."

What is a "Work Made for Hire"? A "work made for hire" is defined as: (1) "a work prepared by an employee within the scope of his or her employment"; or (2)

"a work specially ordered or commissioned for use as a contribution to a collective work, as a part of a motion picture or other audiovisual work, as a translation, as a supplementary work, as a compilation, as an instructional text, as a test, as answer material for a test, or as an atlas, if the parties expressly agree in a written instrument signed by them that the work shall be considered a work made for hire." If you have checked "Yes" to indicate that the work was "made for hire," you must give the full legal name of the employer (or other person for whom the work was prepared). You may also include the name of the employee along with the name of the employer (for example: "Elster Record Co., employer for hire of John Ferguson").

"Anonymous" or "Pseudonymous" Work: An author's contribution to a work is "anonymous" if that author is not identified on the copies or phonorecords of the work. An author's contribution to a work is "pseudonymous" if that author is identified on the copies or phonorecords under a fictitious name. If the work is "anonymous" you may: (1) leave the line blank; or (2) state "anonymous" on the line; or (3) reveal the author's identity. If the work is "pseudonymous" you may: (1) leave the line blank; or (2) give the pseudonym and identify it as such (for example: "Huntley Haverstock, pseudonym"); or (3) reveal the author's name, making clear which is the real name and which is the pseudonym (for example: "Judith Barton, whose pseudonym is Madeline Elster"). However, the citizenship or domicile of the author must be given in all cases.

Dates of Birth and Death: If the author is dead, the statute requires that the year of death be included in the application unless the work is anonymous or pseudonymous. The author's birth date is optional, but is useful as a form of identification. Leave this space blank if the author's contribution was a "work made for hire."

Author's Nationality or Domicile: Give the country in which the author is a citizen, or the country in which the author is domiciled. Nationality or domicile must be given in all cases.

Nature of Authorship: Sound recording authorship is the performance, sound production, or both, that is fixed in the recording deposited for registration. Describe this authorship in space 2 as "sound recording." If the claim also covers the underlying work(s), include the appropriate authorship terms for each author, for example, "words," "music," "arrangement of music," or "text."

Generally, for the claim to cover both the sound recording and the underlying work(s), every author should have contributed to both the sound recording and the underlying work(s). If the claim includes artwork or photographs, include the appropriate term in the statement of authorship.

SPACE 3: Creation and Publication

General Instructions: Do not confuse "creation" with "publication." Every application for copyright registration must state "the year in which creation of the work was completed." Give the date and nation of first publication only if the work has been published.

Creation: Under the statute, a work is "created" when it is fixed in a copy or phonorecord for the first time. Where a work has been prepared over a period of time, the part of the work existing in fixed form on a particular date constitutes the created work on that date. The date you give here should be the year in which the author completed the particular version for which registration is now being sought, even if other versions exist or if further changes or additions are planned.

Publication: The statute defines "publication" as "the distribution of copies or phonorecords of a work to the public by sale or other transfer of ownership, or by rental, lease, or lending"; a work is also "published" if there has been an "offering to distribute copies or phonorecords to a group of persons for purposes of further distribution, public performance, or public display." Give the full date (month, date, year) when, and the country where, publication first occurred. If first publication took place simultaneously in the United States and other countries, it is sufficient to state "U.S.A."

SPACE 4: Claimant(s)

Name(s) and Address(es) of Copyright Claimant(s): Give the name(s) and address(es) of the copyright claimant(s) in the work even if the claimant is the same as the author. Copyright in a work belongs initially to the author of the work (including, in the case of a work made for hire, the employer or other person for whom the work was prepared). The copyright claimant is either the author of the work or a person or organization to whom the copyright initially belonging to the author has been transferred.

Transfer: The statute provides that, if the copyright claimant is not the author, the application for registration must contain "a brief statement of how the claimant obtained ownership of the copyright." If any copyright claimant named in space 4a is not an author named in space 2, give a brief statement explaining how the claimant(s) obtained ownership of the copyright. Examples: "By written contract"; "Transfer of all rights by author"; "Assignment"; "By will." Do not attach transfer documents or other attachments or riders.

SPACE 5: Previous Registration

General Instructions: The questions in space 5 are intended to show whether an earlier registration has been made for this work and, if so, whether there is any basis for a new registration. As a rule, only one basic copyright registration can be made for the same version of a particular work.

Same Version: If this version is substantially the same as the work covered by a previous registration, a second registration is not generally possible unless: (1) the work has been registered in unpublished form and a second registration is now being sought to cover this first published edition; or (2) someone other than the author is identified as copyright claimant in the earlier registration and the author is now seeking registration in his or her own name. If either of these two exceptions applies, check the appropriate box and give the earlier registration number and date. Otherwise, do not submit Form SR. Instead, write the Copyright Office for information about supplementary registration or recordation of transfers of copyright ownership.

Changed Version: If the work has been changed and you are now seeking registration to cover the additions or revisions, check the last box in space 5, give the earlier registration number and date, and complete both parts of space 6 in accordance with the instructions below.

Previous Registration Number and Date: If more than one previous registration has been made for the work, give the number and date of the latest registration.

SPACE 6: Derivative Work or Compilation

General Instructions: Complete space 6 if this work is a "changed version," "compilation," or "derivative work," and if it incorporates one or more earlier works that have already been published or registered for copyright, or that have fallen into the public domain, or sound recordings that were fixed before February 15, 1972. A "compilation" is defined as "a work formed by the collection and assembling of preexisting materials or of data that are selected, coordinated, or arranged in such a way that the resulting work as a whole constitutes an original work of authorship." A "derivative work" is "a work based on one or more preexisting works." Examples of derivative works include recordings reissued with substantial editorial revisions or abridgments of the recorded sounds, and recordings republished with new recorded material, or "any other form in which a work may be recast, transformed, or adapted." Derivative works also include works "consisting of editorial revisions, annotations, or other modifications" if these changes, as a whole, represent an original work of authorship.

Preexisting Material (space 6a): Complete this space and space 6b for derivative works. In this space identify the preexisting work that has been recast, transformed, or adapted. The preexisting work may be material that has been previously published, previously registered, or that is in the public domain. For example, the preexisting material might be: "1970 recording by Sperryville Symphony of Bach Double Concerto."

Material Added to This Work (space 6b): Give a brief, general statement of the **additional** new material covered by the copyright claim for which registration is sought. In the case of a derivative work, identify this new material. Examples: "Recorded performances on bands 1 and 3"; "Remixed sounds from original multitrack sound sources"; "New words, arrangement, and additional sounds." If the work is a compilation, give a brief, general statement describing both the material that has been compiled and the compilation itself. Example: "Compilation of 1938 Recordings by various swing bands."

SPACE 7,8,9: Fee, Correspondence, Certification, Return Address

Deposit Account: If you maintain a Deposit Account in the Copyright Office, identify it in space 7a. Otherwise, leave the space blank and send the filing fee of $30 (effective through June 30, 2002) with your application and deposit. (See space 8 on form.)

Correspondence (space 7b): This space should contain the name, address, area code, telephone number, fax number, and email address (if available) of the person to be consulted if correspondence about this application becomes necessary.

Certification (space 8): This application cannot be accepted unless it bears the date and the **handwritten signature** of the author or other copyright claimant, or of the owner of exclusive right(s), or of the duly authorized agent of the author, claimant, or owner of exclusive right(s).

Address for Return of Certificate (space 9): The address box must be completed legibly since the certificate will be returned in a window envelope.

MORE INFORMATION

"Works": "Works" are the basic subject matter of copyright; they are what authors create and copyright protects. The statute draws a sharp distinction between the "work" and "any material object in which the work is embodied."

"Copies" and "Phonorecords": These are the two types of material objects in which "works" are embodied. In general, "copies" are objects from which a work can be read or visually perceived, directly or with the aid of a machine or device, such as manuscripts, books, sheet music, film, and videotape. **"Phonorecords"** are objects embodying fixations of sounds, such as audio tapes and phonograph disks. For example, a song (the "work") can be reproduced in sheet music ("copies") or phonograph disks ("phonorecords"), or both.

"Sound Recordings": These are "works," not "copies" or "phonorecords." "Sound recordings" are "works that result from the fixation of a series of musical, spoken, or other sounds, but not including the sounds accompanying a motion picture or other audiovisual work." Example: When a record company issues a new release, the release will typically involve two distinct "works": the "musical work" that has been recorded, and the "sound recording" as a separate work in itself. The material objects that the record company sends out are "phonorecords": physical reproductions of both the "musical work" and the "sound recording."

Should You File More Than One Application? If your work consists of a recorded musical, dramatic, or literary work and if both the "work" and the sound recording as a separate "work" are eligible for registration, the application form you should file depends on the following:

File Only Form SR if: The copyright claimant is the same for both the musical, dramatic, or literary work and for the sound recording, and you are seeking a single registration to cover both of these "works."

File Only Form PA (or Form TX) if: You are seeking to register only the musical, dramatic, or literary work, not the sound recording. Form PA is appropriate for works of the performing arts; Form TX is for nondramatic literary works.

Separate Applications Should Be Filed on Form PA (or Form TX) and on Form SR if: (1) The copyright claimant for the musical, dramatic, or literary work is different from the copyright claimant for the sound recording; or (2) You prefer to have separate registrations for the musical, dramatic, or literary work and for the sound recording.

127

Copyright
SR (Sound Recordings)

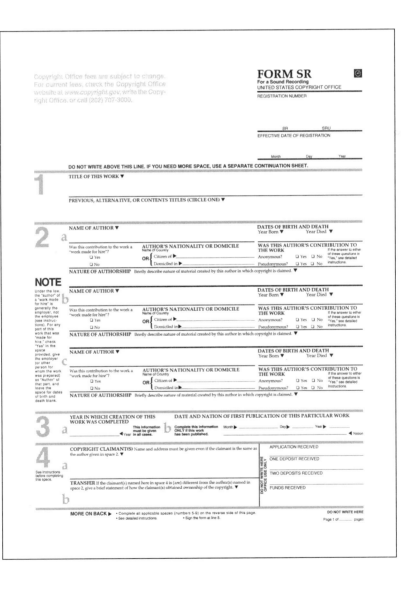

EXAMINED BY	FORM SR
CHECKED BY	
CORRESPONDENCE ☐ Yes	FOR COPYRIGHT OFFICE USE ONLY

DO NOT WRITE ABOVE THIS LINE. IF YOU NEED MORE SPACE, USE A SEPARATE CONTINUATION SHEET.

PREVIOUS REGISTRATION Has registration for this work, or for an earlier version of this work, already been made in the Copyright Office?
☐ Yes ☐ No If your answer is "Yes," why is another registration being sought? (Check appropriate box) ▼
a. ☐ This work was previously registered in unpublished form and now has been published for the first time.
b. ☐ This is the first application submitted by this author as copyright claimant.
c. ☐ This is a changed version of the work, as shown by space 6 on this application.
If your answer is "Yes," give: **Previous Registration Number ▼**   **Year of Registration ▼**

5

DERIVATIVE WORK OR COMPILATION
Preexisting Material Identify any preexisting work or works that this work is based on or incorporates. ▼

a

Material Added to This Work Give a brief, general statement of the material that has been added to this work and in which copyright is claimed. ▼

b

6

See instructions before completing this space.

DEPOSIT ACCOUNT If the registration fee is to be charged to a Deposit Account established in the Copyright Office, give name and number of Account.
Name ▼   **Account Number ▼**

a

CORRESPONDENCE Give name and address to which correspondence about this application should be sent.   Name/Address/Apt/City/State/ZIP ▼

b

Area code and daytime telephone number   Fax number
Email

7

CERTIFICATION* I, the undersigned, hereby certify that I am the
Check only one ▼
☐ author
☐ other copyright claimant
☐ owner of exclusive right(s)
☐ authorized agent of _____
                    Name of author or other copyright claimant, or owner of exclusive right(s) ▲

of the work identified in this application and that the statements made by me in this application are correct to the best of my knowledge.
Typed or printed name and date ▼ If this application gives a date of publication in space 3, do not sign and submit it before that date.
                                                                            Date _____

Handwritten signature (x) ▼
X _____

8

Certificate will be mailed in window envelope to this address	Name ▼
	Number/Street/Apt ▼
	City/State/ZIP ▼

YOU MUST:
• Complete all necessary spaces
• Sign your application in space 8
SEND ALL 3 ELEMENTS IN THE SAME PACKAGE:
1. Application form
2. Nonrefundable filing fee in check or money order payable to Register of Copyrights
3. Deposit material
MAIL TO:
Library of Congress
Copyright Office
101 Independence Avenue, S.E.
Washington, D.C. 20559-6000

Fees are subject to change. For current fees, check the Copyright Office website at www.copyright.gov, write the Copyright Office, or call (202) 707-3000.

9

*17 U.S.C. § 506(e): Any person who knowingly makes a false representation of a material fact in the application for copyright registration provided for by section 409, or in any written statement filed in connection with the application, shall be fined not more than $2,500.

Rev: June 2002—20,000   Web Rev: June 2002   ♻ Printed on recycled paper   U.S. Government Printing Office: 2000-461-113/20,021

Copyright
VA (Visual Arts)

Copyright Office fees are subject to change. For current fees, check the Copyright Office website at www.copyright.gov, write the Copyright Office, or call (202) 707-3000.

FORM VA
For a Work of the Visual Arts
UNITED STATES COPYRIGHT OFFICE

REGISTRATION NUMBER

VA   VAU

EFFECTIVE DATE OF REGISTRATION

Month   Day   Year

DO NOT WRITE ABOVE THIS LINE. IF YOU NEED MORE SPACE, USE A SEPARATE CONTINUATION SHEET.

1 Title of This Work ▼   NATURE OF THIS WORK ▼ See instructions

Previous or Alternative Titles ▼

Publication as a Contribution If this work was published as a contribution to a periodical, serial, or collection, give information about the collective work in which the contribution appeared. Title of Collective Work ▼

If published in a periodical or serial give: Volume ▼   Number ▼   Issue Date ▼   On Pages ▼

2 NAME OF AUTHOR ▼   DATES OF BIRTH AND DEATH
Year Born ▼   Year Died ▼

NOTE
Under the law, the "author" of a "work made for hire" is generally the employer, not the employee (see instructions). For any part of this work that was "made for hire" check "Yes" in the space provided, give the employer (or other person for whom the work was prepared) as "Author" of that part, and leave the space for dates of birth and death blank.

Was this contribution to the work a "work made for hire"?
☐ Yes
☐ No

Author's Nationality or Domicile
Name of Country
OR { Citizen of _____
Domiciled in _____

Was This Author's Contribution to the Work
Anonymous?   ☐ Yes ☐ No   If the answer to either
Pseudonymous?   ☐ Yes ☐ No   of these questions is "Yes," see detailed instructions.

Nature of Authorship Check appropriate box(es). See instructions
☐ 3-Dimensional sculpture   ☐ Map   ☐ Technical drawing
☐ 2-Dimensional artwork   ☐ Photograph   ☐ Text
☐ Reproduction of work of art   ☐ Jewelry design   ☐ Architectural work

Name of Author ▼   Dates of Birth and Death
Year Born ▼   Year Died ▼

Was this contribution to the work a "work made for hire"?
☐ Yes
☐ No

Author's Nationality or Domicile
Name of Country
OR { Citizen of _____
Domiciled in _____

Was This Author's Contribution to the Work
Anonymous?   ☐ Yes ☐ No   If the answer to either
Pseudonymous?   ☐ Yes ☐ No   of these questions is "Yes," see detailed instructions.

Nature of Authorship Check appropriate box(es). See instructions
☐ 3-Dimensional sculpture   ☐ Map   ☐ Technical drawing
☐ 2-Dimensional artwork   ☐ Photograph   ☐ Text
☐ Reproduction of work of art   ☐ Jewelry design   ☐ Architectural work

3 Year in Which Creation of This Work Was Completed
This information must be given Year in all cases.

Date and Nation of First Publication of This Particular Work
Complete this information ONLY if this work has been published.
Month _____ Day _____ Year _____
Nation

4 COPYRIGHT CLAIMANT(S) Name and address must be given even if the claimant is the same as the author given in space 2. ▼

Transfer If the claimant(s) named here in space 4 is (are) different from the author(s) named in space 2, give a brief statement of how the claimant(s) obtained ownership of the copyright. ▼

DO NOT WRITE HERE OFFICE USE ONLY

APPLICATION RECEIVED

ONE DEPOSIT RECEIVED

TWO DEPOSITS RECEIVED

FUNDS RECEIVED

MORE ON BACK ▶ • Complete all applicable spaces (numbers 5-9) on the reverse side of this page
• See detailed instructions.   • Sign the form at line 8.

DO NOT WRITE HERE
Page 1 of _____ pages

	EXAMINED BY	FORM VA
	CHECKED BY	
	☐ CORRESPONDENCE Yes	FOR COPYRIGHT OFFICE USE ONLY

DO NOT WRITE ABOVE THIS LINE. IF YOU NEED MORE SPACE, USE A SEPARATE CONTINUATION SHEET.

PREVIOUS REGISTRATION Has registration for this work, or for an earlier version of this work, already been made in the Copyright Office?

☐ **Yes** ☐ **No** If your answer is "Yes," why is another registration being sought? (Check appropriate box.) ▼

a. ☐ This is the first published edition of a work previously registered in unpublished form.

b. ☐ This is the first application submitted by this author as copyright claimant.

c. ☐ This is a changed version of the work, as shown by space 6 on this application.

If your answer is "Yes." give: **Previous Registration Number** ▼   **Year of Registration** ▼

5

DERIVATIVE WORK OR COMPILATION Complete both space 6a and 6b for a derivative work; complete only 6b for a compilation.

a. **Preexisting Material** Identify any preexisting work or works that this work is based on or incorporates. ▼

b. **Material Added to This Work** Give a brief, general statement of the material that has been added to this work and in which copyright is claimed. ▼

6

a

See instructions before completing this space.

b

DEPOSIT ACCOUNT If the registration fee is to be charged to a Deposit Account established in the Copyright Office, give name and number of Account.

Name ▼   **Account Number** ▼

7

a

CORRESPONDENCE Give name and address to which correspondence about this application should be sent. Name/Address/Apt/City/State/ZIP ▼

b

Area code and daytime telephone number   (   )   Fax number   (   )

Email

CERTIFICATION* I, the undersigned, hereby certify that I am the

check only one ▶

☐ author
☐ other copyright claimant
☐ owner of exclusive right(s)
☐ authorized agent of _____
  Name of author or other copyright claimant, or owner of exclusive right(s) ▲

of the work identified in this application and that the statements made by me in this application are correct to the best of my knowledge.

Typed or printed name and date ▼ If this application gives a date of publication in space 3, do not sign and submit it before that date.

_____ Date _____

Handwritten signature (X) ▼

X _____

8

Certificate will be mailed in window envelope to this address:	Name ▼
	Number/Street/Apt ▼
	City/State/ZIP ▼

YOU MUST:
• Complete all necessary spaces
• Sign your application in space 8
SEND ALL 3 ELEMENTS IN THE SAME PACKAGE:
1. Application form
2. Nonrefundable filing fee in check or money order payable to Register of Copyrights
3. Deposit material
MAIL TO:
Library of Congress
Copyright Office
101 Independence Avenue, S.E.
Washington, D.C. 20559-6000

Fees are subject to change. For current fees, check the Copyright Office website at www.copyright.gov, write the Copyright Office, or call (202) 707-3000.

9

Rev: June 2002—20,000 Web Rev: June 2002 ♲ Printed on recycled paper   U.S. Government Printing Office: 2000-461-113/20,021

Copyright
VA Short Form

🖉 Instructions for Short Form VA 🖉

For pictorial, graphic, and sculptural works

USE THIS FORM IF—

1. You are the **only** author and copyright owner of this work, *and*
2. The work was **not** made for hire, *and*
3. The work is completely new (does not contain a substantial amount of material that has been previously published or registered or is in the public domain).

If any of the above does not apply, you must use standard Form VA.
NOTE: *Short Form VA is not appropriate for an anonymous author who does not wish to reveal his or her identity.*

HOW TO COMPLETE SHORT FORM VA

- Type or print in black ink.
- Be clear and legible. (Your certificate of registration will be copied from your form.)
- Give only the information requested.

NOTE: You may use a continuation sheet (Form __/CON) to list individual titles in a collection. Complete Space A and list the individual titles under Space C on the back page. Space B is not applicable to short forms.

1 Title of This Work

You must give a title. If there is no title, state "UNTITLED." If you are registering an unpublished collection, give the collection title you want to appear in our records (for example: "Jewelry by Josephine, 1995 Volume"). Alternative title: If the work is known by two titles, you also may give the second title. If the work has been published as part of a larger work (including a periodical), give the title of that larger work instead of an alternative title, in addition to the title of the contribution.

2 Name and Address of Author and Owner of the Copyright

Give your name and mailing address. You may include your pseudonym followed by "pseud." Also, give the nation of which you are a citizen or where you have your domicile (i.e., permanent residence). Please give daytime phone, fax numbers, and email address, if available.

3 Year of Creation

Give the latest year in which you completed the work you are registering at this time. A work is "created" when it is "fixed" in a tangible form. Examples: drawn on paper, molded in clay, stored in a computer.

4 Publication

If the work has been published (i.e., if copies have been distributed to the public), give the complete date of publication (month, day, and year) and the nation where the publication first took place.

5 Type of Authorship in This Work

Check the box or boxes that describe your authorship in the material you are sending. For example, if you are registering illustrations but have not written the story yet, check only the box for "2-dimensional artwork."

6 Signature of Author

Sign the application in black ink and check the appropriate box. The person signing the application should be the author or his/her authorized agent.

7 Person to Contact for Rights/Permissions

This space is optional. You may give the name and address of the person or organization to contact for permission to use the work. You may also provide phone, fax, or email information.

8 Certificate Will Be Mailed

This space must be completed. Your certificate of registration will be mailed in a window envelope to this address. Also, if the Copyright Office needs to contact you, we will write to this address.

9 Deposit Account

Complete this space only if you currently maintain a deposit account in the Copyright Office.

▓▓ MAIL WITH THE FORM ▓▓

- A $30 filing fee (Copyright Office fees are subject to change. For current fees, please check the Copyright Office website at *www.copyright.gov*, write the Copyright Office, or call (202) 707-3000.) in the form of a check or money order (*no cash*) payable to "Register of Copyrights," **and**
- One or two copies of the work or identifying material consisting of photographs or drawings showing the work. See table (right) for the requirements for most works. **Note:** Request Circular 40a for more information about the requirements for other works. Copies submitted become the property of the U.S. Government.

Mail everything (**application form, copy or copies, and fee**) *in one package* to:

Library of Congress
Copyright Office
101 Independence Avenue, S.E.
Washington, D.C. 20559-6000

QUESTIONS? Call (202) 707-3000 [TTY: (202) 707-6737] between 8:30 a.m. and 5:00 p.m. eastern time, Monday through Friday. For forms and informational circulars, call (202) 707-9100 24 hours a day, 7 days a week, or download them from the Copyright Office website at *www.copyright.gov*. Selected informational circulars but not forms are available from Fax-on-Demand at (202) 707-2600.

If you are registering:	And the work is *unpublished/published* send:
2-dimensional artwork in a book, map, poster, or print	**a.** And the work is *unpublished*, send one complete copy or identifying material **b.** And the work is *published*, send two copies of the best published edition
• 3-dimensional sculpture, • 2-dimensional artwork applied to a T-shirt	**a.** And the work is *unpublished*, send identifying material **b.** And the work is *published*, send identifying material
• a greeting card, pattern, commercial print or label, fabric, wallpaper	**a.** And the work is *unpublished*, send one complete copy or identifying material **b.** And the work is *published*, send one copy of the best published edition

PRIVACY ACT ADVISORY STATEMENT Required by the Privacy Act of 1974 (P.L. 93-579)
The authority for requesting this information is title 17 U.S.C., secs. 409 and 410. Furnishing the requested information is voluntary. But if the information is not furnished, it may be necessary to delay or refuse registration and you may not be entitled to certain relief, remedies, and benefits provided in chapters 4 and 5 of title 17 U.S.C.
The principal uses of the requested information are the establishment and maintenance of a public record and the examination of the application for compliance with the registration requirements of the copyright law.
Other routine uses include public inspection and copying, preparation of public indexes, preparation of public catalogs of copyright registrations, and preparation of search reports upon request.
NOTE: No other advisory statement will be given in connection with this application. Please keep this statement and refer to it if we communicate with you regarding this application.

Copyright Office fees are subject to change. For current fees, check the Copyright Office website at *www.copyright.gov*, write the Copyright Office, or call (202) 707-3000.

Short Form VA
For a Work of the Visual Arts
UNITED STATES COPYRIGHT OFFICE

Registration Number

VA   VAU

Effective Date of Registration

Application Received

Deposit Received
One   Two

Fee Received

Examined By

Correspondence ☐

TYPE OR PRINT IN BLACK INK. DO NOT WRITE ABOVE THIS LINE.

Title of This Work: Alternative title or title of larger work in which this work was published:	**1**	
Name and Address of Author and Owner of the Copyright: Nationality or domicile: Phone, fax, and email:	**2**	Phone ( ) Fax ( ) Email
Year of Creation:	**3**	
If work has been published, Date and Nation of Publication:	**4**	a. Date _____ Month _____ Day _____ Year ____ *(Month, day, and year all required)* b. Nation
Type of Authorship in This Work: Check all that this author created.	**5**	☐ 3-Dimensional sculpture ☐ Photograph ☐ Map ☐ 2-Dimensional artwork ☐ Jewelry design ☐ Text ☐ Technical drawing
Signature: Registration cannot be completed without a signature.	**6**	*I certify that the statements made by me in this application are correct to the best of my knowledge.* **Check one:** ☐ Author ☐ Authorized agent X _____
OPTIONAL **Name and Address of Person to Contact for Rights and Permissions:** Phone, fax, and email:	**7**	☐ Check here if same as #2 above. Phone ( ) Fax ( ) Email

8 Certificate will be mailed in window envelope to this address:

Name ▼

Number/Street/Apt ▼

City/State/ZIP ▼

Complete this space only if you currently hold a Deposit Account in the Copyright Office.

9 Deposit Account #_____

Name _____

DO NOT WRITE HERE   Page 1 of ___ pages

*17 U.S.C. § 506(e): Any person who knowingly makes a false representation of a material fact in the application for copyright registration provided for by section 409, or in any written statement filed in connection with the application, shall be fined not more than $2,500.

Rev: June 2002—20,000   Web Rev: June 2002   ♻ Printed on recycled paper

U.S. Government Printing Office: 2000-461-113/20,021

133

Copyright
Continuation Sheet

CONTINUATION SHEET
FOR APPLICATION FORMS

ⓒ**FORM** ____ **/CON**
UNITED STATES COPYRIGHT OFFICE

REGISTRATION NUMBER

- This Continuation Sheet is used in conjunction with Forms CA, PA, SE, SR, TX, and VA, **only**. Indicate which basic form you are continuing in the space in the upper right-hand corner.
- If at all possible, try to fit the information called for into the spaces provided on the basic form.
- If you do not have enough space for all the information you need to give on the basic form, use this Continuation Sheet and submit it with the basic form.
- If you submit this Continuation Sheet, clip (do not tape or staple) it to the basic form and fold the two together before submitting them.
- Space A of this sheet is intended to identify the basic application.
  Space B is a continuation of Space 2 on the basic application. Space B is not applicable to Short Forms.
  Space C (on the reverse side of this sheet) is for the continuation of Spaces 1, 4, or 6 on the basic application or for the continuation of Space 1 on any of the three Short Forms PA, TX, or VA.

PA	PAU	SE	SEG	SEU	SR	SRU	TX	TXU	VA	VAU

EFFECTIVE DATE OF REGISTRATION

_____ (Month) _____ (Day) _____ (Year)
CONTINUATION SHEET RECEIVED

Page _____ of _____ pages

DO NOT WRITE ABOVE THIS LINE. FOR COPYRIGHT OFFICE USE ONLY

A
Identification
of
Application

IDENTIFICATION OF CONTINUATION SHEET: This sheet is a continuation of the application for copyright registration on the basic form submitted for the following work:
- TITLE: (Give the title as given under the heading "Title of this Work" in Space 1 of the basic form.)

- NAME(S) AND ADDRESS(ES) OF COPYRIGHT CLAIMANT(S). (Give the name and address of at least one copyright claimant as given in Space 4 of the basic form or Space 2 of any of the Short Forms PA, TX, or VA.)

B
Continuation
of Space 2

d

NAME OF AUTHOR ▼

DATES OF BIRTH AND DEATH
Year Born▼   Year Died▼

Was this contribution to the work a "work made for hire"?
❏ Yes
❏ No

AUTHOR'S NATIONALITY OR DOMICILE
Name of Country
OR { Citizen of ▶ _____
{ Domiciled in ▶ _____

WAS THIS AUTHOR'S CONTRIBUTION TO THE WORK
Anonymous? ❏ Yes ❏ No
Pseudonymous? ❏ Yes ❏ No
If the answer to either of these questions is "Yes," see detailed instructions.

NATURE OF AUTHORSHIP Briefly describe nature of the material created by the author in which copyright is claimed. ▼

e

NAME OF AUTHOR ▼

DATES OF BIRTH AND DEATH
Year Born▼   Year Died▼

Was this contribution to the work a "work made for hire"?
❏ Yes
❏ No

AUTHOR'S NATIONALITY OR DOMICILE
Name of Country
OR { Citizen of ▶ _____
{ Domiciled in ▶ _____

WAS THIS AUTHOR'S CONTRIBUTION TO THE WORK
Anonymous? ❏ Yes ❏ No
Pseudonymous? ❏ Yes ❏ No
If the answer to either of these questions is "Yes," see detailed instructions.

NATURE OF AUTHORSHIP Briefly describe nature of the material created by the author in which copyright is claimed. ▼

f

NAME OF AUTHOR ▼

DATES OF BIRTH AND DEATH
Year Born▼   Year Died▼

Was this contribution to the work a "work made for hire"?
❏ Yes
❏ No

AUTHOR'S NATIONALITY OR DOMICILE
Name of Country
OR { Citizen of ▶ _____
{ Domiciled in ▶ _____

WAS THIS AUTHOR'S CONTRIBUTION TO THE WORK
Anonymous? ❏ Yes ❏ No
Pseudonymous? ❏ Yes ❏ No
If the answer to either of these questions is "Yes," see detailed instructions.

NATURE OF AUTHORSHIP Briefly describe nature of the material created by the author in which copyright is claimed. ▼

Use the reverse side of this sheet if you need more space for continuation of Spaces 1, 4, or 6 of the basic form or for the continuation of Space 1 on any of the Short Forms PA, TX, or VA.

CONTINUATION OF (Check which): ❑ Space 1 ❑ Space 4 ❑ Space 6

C

Continuation
of other
Spaces

Certificate
will be
mailed in
window
envelope
to this
address:

Name ▼

Number/Street/Apt ▼

City/State/ZIP ▼

YOU MUST:
• Complete all necessary spaces
• Sign your application

SEND ALL 3 ELEMENTS
IN THE SAME PACKAGE:
1. Application form
2. Nonrefundable fee in check or
money order payable to *Register
of Copyrights*
3. Deposit Material

MAIL TO:
Library of Congress, Copyright Office
101 Independence Avenue, S.E.
Washington, D.C. 20559-6000

D

Fees are subject to
change. For current
fees, check the
Copyright Office
website at
www.copyright.gov,
write the Copyright
Office, or call
(202) 707-3000.

Rev: June 2002—20,000   Web Rev: June 2002   ♻ Printed on recycled paper

U.S. Government Printing Office: 2000-461-113/20,021

Copyright
CA (Corrections of Application)

☑ Form CA ☑

Detach and read these instructions before completing this form.
Make sure all applicable spaces have been filled in before you return this form.

BASIC INFORMATION

Use Form CA When:
An earlier registration has been completed in the Copyright Office; and
• Some of the facts given in that registration are incorrect or incomplete; and
• You want to place the correct or complete facts on record.

Purpose of Supplementary Copyright Registration: As a rule, only one basic copyright registration can be made for the same work. To take care of cases where information in the basic registration turns out to be incorrect or incomplete, section 408(d) of the copyright law provides for "the filing of an application for supplementary registration, to correct an error in a copyright registration or to amplify the information given in a registration."

Who May File: Once basic registration has been made for a work, any author or other copyright claimant or owner of any exclusive right in the work or the duly authorized agent of any such author, other claimant, or owner who wishes to correct or amplify the information given in the basic registration may submit Form CA.

Please Note: Do not use Form CA to correct errors in statements on the copies or phonorecords of the work in question or to reflect changes in the content of the work. If the work has been changed substantially, you should consider making an entirely new registration for the revised version to cover the additions or revisions.

Do not use Form CA as a substitute for renewal registration. Renewal of copyright cannot be accomplished by using Form CA. For information on renewal of copyright, request Circular 15, "Renewal of Copyright," from the Copyright Office. Do not use Form CA to correct an error regarding publication when the work was registered as an unpublished work.

Do not use Form CA as a substitute for recording a transfer of copyright or other document pertaining to rights under a copyright. Recording a document under section 205 of the statute gives all persons constructive notice of the facts stated in the document and may have other important consequences in cases of infringement or conflicting transfers. Supplementary registration does not have that legal effect.

For information on recording a document, request Circular 12, "Recordation of Transfers and Other Documents," from the Copyright Office. To record a document in the Copyright Office, request the Document Cover Sheet.

How to Apply for Supplementary Registration:
First: Study the information on this page to make sure that filing an application on Form CA is the best procedure to follow in your case.
Second: Read the back of this page for specific instructions on filling out Form CA. Before starting to complete the form, make sure that you have all the necessary detailed information from the certificate of the basic registration.

Third: Complete all applicable spaces on the form following the line-by-line instructions on the back of this page. Use a typewriter or print the information in black ink.
Fourth: Detach this sheet and send your completed Form CA along with a **photocopy** of the front and back of the certificate of registration being amended to:
Library of Congress
Copyright Office
101 Independence Avenue, S.E.
Washington, D.C. 20559-6000
Fee: Do not send copies, phonorecords, or supporting documents other than the photocopied certificate with your application. They cannot be made part of the record of a supplementary registration. Unless you have a Deposit Account in the Copyright Office, your application must be accompanied by a nonrefundable filing fee in the form of a check or money order for $100* payable to: *Register of Copyrights.*

*NOTE: Copyright Office fees are subject to change. For current fees, check the Copyright Office website at *www.copyright.gov*, write the Copyright Office, or call (202) 707-3000.

What Happens When a Supplementary Registration Is Made? When a supplementary registration is completed, the Copyright Office will assign it a new registration number in the appropriate registration category and will issue a certificate of supplementary registration under that number. The basic registration will not be cancelled. The two registrations will stand in the Copyright Office records. The supplementary registration will have the effect of calling the public's attention to a possible error or omission in the basic registration and of placing the correct facts or the additional information on official record.

For Further Information
• **Internet:** Circulars, application forms, announcements, and other related materials are available at *www.copyright.gov*
• **Fax:** Circulars are available from Fax-on-Demand at (202) 707-2600.
• **Telephone:** To speak to an information specialist, call the Public Information Office at (202) 707-3000 (TTY (202) 707-6737). Recorded information is available 24 hours a day. If you know which application forms and circulars you want, call the Forms and Publications Hotline at (202) 707-9100 24 hours a day.
• **Regular Mail:**
Library of Congress
Copyright Office
Public Information Office
101 Independence Avenue, S.E.
Washington, D.C. 20599-6000

LINE-BY-LINE INSTRUCTIONS

Please type or print neatly using black ink. The certificate of registration is created by copying your CA application form.

 SPACE A: Identification of Basic Registration

General Instructions: The information in this part identifies the basic registration that will be corrected or amplified. Even if the purpose of filing Form CA is to change one of these items, each item must agree exactly with the information as it already appears in the basic registration, that is, as it appears in the registration you wish to correct. Do not give any new information in this part.

Title of Work: Give the title as it appears in the basic registration.

Registration Number: Give the registration number (the series of numbers preceded by one or more letters) that appears in the upper right-hand corner of the certificate of registration. Give only one basic registration number since one CA form may correct or amend only one basic registration.

Registration Date: Give the year when the basic registration was completed.

Name(s) of Author(s) and Copyright Claimant(s): Give all the names as they appear in the basic registration.

 SPACE B: Correction

General Instructions: Complete this part **only** if information in the basic registration **was incorrect at the time that basic registration was made.** Leave this part blank and complete Part C instead if your purpose is to add, update, or clarify information rather than to rectify an actual error.

Location and Nature of Incorrect Information: Give the line number and the heading or description of the space in the basic registration where the error occurs. Example: Line number 2...Citizenship of author.

Incorrect Information as It Appears in Basic Registration: Transcribe the incorrect statement exactly as it appears in the basic registration, even if you have already given this information in Part A.

Corrected Information: Give the statement as it should have appeared in the application of the basic registration.

Explanation of Correction: You may need to add an explanation to clarify this correction.

 SPACE C: Amplification

General Instructions: Complete this part if you want to provide any of the following: (1) information that was omitted at the time of basic registration; (2) changes in facts other than ownership but including changes such as title or address of claimant that have occurred since the basic registration; or (3) explanations clarifying information in the basic registration.

Location and Nature of Information to Be Amplified: Give the line number and the heading or description of the space in the basic registration where the information to be amplified appears.

Amplified Information: Give a statement of the additional, updated, or explanatory information as clearly and succinctly as possible. You should add an explanation of the amplification if it is necessary.

 SPACES D,E,F,G: Continuation, Fee, Certification, Return Address

Continuation (Part D): Use this space if you do not have enough room in Parts B or C.

Deposit Account and Mailing Instructions (Part E): If you maintain a Deposit Account in the Copyright Office, identify it in Part E. Otherwise, you will need to send the nonrefundable filing fee with your form. The space headed "Correspondence" should contain the name, address, telephone number with area code, and fax and email numbers, if available, of the person to be consulted if correspondence about the form becomes necessary.

Certification (Part F): The application is not acceptable unless it bears the handwritten signature of the author, or other copyright claimant, or of the owner of exclusive right(s), or of the duly authorized agent of such author, claimant, or owner.

Address for Return of Certificate (Part G): The address box must be completed legibly, since a reproduced image of that space will appear in the window of the mailing envelope.

137

Copyright

CA (Corrections of Application)

Copyright Office fees are subject to change. For current fees, check the Copyright Office website at www.copyright.gov, write the Copyright Office, or call (202) 707-3000.

FORM CA
For Supplementary Registration
UNITED STATES COPYRIGHT OFFICE

REGISTRATION NUMBER

| TX | TXU | PA | PAU | VA | VAU | SR | SRU | RE |

EFFECTIVE DATE OF SUPPLEMENTARY REGISTRATION

Month   Day   Year

DO NOT WRITE ABOVE THIS LINE. IF YOU NEED MORE SPACE, USE A SEPARATE CONTINUATION SHEET.

A

Title of Work ▼

Registration Number of the Basic Registration ▼

Year of Basic Registration ▼

Name(s) of Author(s) ▼

Name(s) of Copyright Claimant(s) ▼

B

Location and Nature of Incorrect Information in Basic Registration ▼

Line Number _____ Line Heading or Description _____

Incorrect Information as It Appears in Basic Registration ▼

Corrected Information ▼

Explanation of Correction ▼

C

Location and Nature of Information in Basic Registration to be Amplified ▼

Line Number _____ Line Heading or Description _____

Amplified Information and Explanation of Information ▼

MORE ON BACK ▶ • Complete all applicable spaces (D–G) on the reverse side of this page.
• See detailed instructions.   • Sign the form at Space F.

DO NOT WRITE HERE

Page 1 of _____ pages

FORM CA RECEIVED	**FORM CA**
FUNDS RECEIVED DATE	
EXAMINED BY	FOR COPYRIGHT OFFICE USE ONLY
CORRESPONDENCE ❑	
REFERENCE TO THIS REGISTRATION ADDED TO BASIC REGISTRATION ❑ YES ❑ NO	

DO NOT WRITE ABOVE THIS LINE. IF YOU NEED MORE SPACE, USE A SEPARATE CONTINUATION SHEET.

Continuation of: ❑ Part B *or* ❑ Part C

D

Correspondence: Give name and address to which correspondence about this application should be sent.

E

Phone (_____) _____ Fax (_____) _____ Email _____

Deposit Account: If the registration fee is to be charged to a Deposit Account established in the Copyright Office, give name and number of Account.

Name _____

Account Number _____

Certification* I, the undersigned, hereby certify that I am the: (Check only one)

❑ author
❑ other copyright claimant
❑ owner of exclusive right(s)
❑ duly authorized agent of _____
Name of author or other copyright claimant, or owner of exclusive right(s) ▲

of the work identified in this application and that the statements made by me in this application are correct to the best of my knowledge.

Typed or printed name ▼   Date ▼

Handwritten signature (X) ▼

F

Certificate will be mailed in window envelope to this address:	Name ▼	YOU MUST: • Complete all necessary spaces • Sign your application in Space F
	Number/Street/Apt ▼	SEND ALL ELEMENTS IN THE SAME PACKAGE: 1. Application form 2. Nonrefundable filing fee in check or money order payable to *Register of Copyrights*
	City/State/ZIP ▼	MAIL TO: Library of Congress Copyright Office 101 Independence Avenue, S.E. Washington, D.C. 20559-6000

G

*17 U.S.C. § 506(e): Any person who knowingly makes a false representation of a material fact in the application for copyright registration provided for by section 409, or in any written statement filed in connection with the application, shall be fined not more than $2,500.

Rev: June 2002—20,000   Web Rev: June 2002   ♻ Printed on recycled paper   U.S. Government Printing Office: 2000-461-113/20,021

Copyright
RE (Renewal)

Copyright Office fees are subject to change. For current fees, check the Copyright Office website at www.copyright.gov, write the Copyright Office, or call (202) 707-3000.

FORM RE
For Renewal of a Work
UNITED STATES COPYRIGHT OFFICE

REGISTRATION NUMBER

EFFECTIVE DATE OF RENEWAL REGISTRATION

| Month | Day | Year |

DO NOT WRITE ABOVE THIS LINE. IF YOU NEED MORE SPACE, USE A SEPARATE CONTINUATION SHEET (FORM RE/CON).

1 RENEWAL CLAIMANT(S), ADDRESS(ES), AND STATEMENT OF CLAIM ▼ (See Instructions)

a
Name ....
Address ....
Claiming as ....
(Use appropriate statement from instructions)

b
Name ....
Address ....
Claiming as ....

c
Name ....
Address ....
Claiming as ....

2 TITLE OF WORK IN WHICH RENEWAL IS CLAIMED ▼

RENEWABLE MATTER ▼

PUBLICATION AS A CONTRIBUTION If this work was published as a contribution to a periodical, serial, or other composite work, give information about the collective work in which the contribution appeared. **Title of Collective Work ▼**

If published in a periodical or serial give: Volume ▼   Number ▼   Issue Date ▼

3 AUTHOR(S) OF RENEWABLE MATTER ▼

4 ORIGINAL REGISTRATION NUMBER ▼   ORIGINAL COPYRIGHT CLAIMANT ▼

ORIGINAL DATE OF COPYRIGHT

If the original registration for this work was made in published form, give:
DATE OF PUBLICATION: _____
(Month)   (Day)   (Year)

OR

If the original registration for this work was made in unpublished form, give:
DATE OF REGISTRATION: _____
(Month)   (Day)   (Year)

MORE ON BACK ▶ ◀ Complete all applicable spaces (numbers 5–8) on the reverse side of this page.   • See detailed instructions.   • Sign the form at space 7.

DO NOT WRITE HERE
Page 1 of _____ pages

RENEWAL APPLICATION RECEIVED	FORM RE
CORRESPONDENCE ☐ YES	
EXAMINED BY	FOR COPYRIGHT OFFICE USE ONLY
CHECKED BY	
FUNDS RECEIVED	

DO NOT WRITE ABOVE THIS LINE. IF YOU NEED MORE SPACE, USE A SEPARATE CONTINUATION SHEET (FORM RE/CON).

RENEWAL FOR GROUP OF WORKS BY SAME AUTHOR: To make a single registration for a group of works by the same individual author published as contributions to periodicals (see instructions), give full information about each contribution. If more space is needed, request continuation sheet (Form RE/CON).

5

a
Title of Contribution: ....
Title of Periodical: ....
Vol: .... No: .... Issue Date: ....
Date of Publication: .... (Month) (Day) (Year)
Registration Number: ....

b
Title of Contribution: ....
Title of Periodical: ....
Vol: .... No: .... Issue Date: ....
Date of Publication: .... (Month) (Day) (Year)
Registration Number: ....

c
Title of Contribution: ....
Title of Periodical: ....
Vol: .... No: .... Issue Date: ....
Date of Publication: .... (Month) (Day) (Year)
Registration Number: ....

d
Title of Contribution: ....
Title of Periodical: ....
Vol: .... No: .... Issue Date: ....
Date of Publication: .... (Month) (Day) (Year)
Registration Number: ....

DEPOSIT ACCOUNT: If the registration fee is to be charged to a Deposit Account established in the Copyright Office, give name and number of Account.

Name _____

Account Number _____

Area code and daytime telephone number ▶ _____

CORRESPONDENCE: Give name and address to which correspondence about this application should be sent.

Name _____

Address _____ (Apt)

(City) (State) (ZIP)

Fax number ▶ _____ Email Address ▶ _____

6

CERTIFICATION* I, the undersigned, hereby certify that I am the: (Check one)
☐ renewal claimant   ☐ duly authorized agent of _____ (Name of renewal claimant) ▲
of the work identified in this application and that the statements made by me in this application are correct to the best of my knowledge.

Typed or printed name ▼ _____ Date ▼ _____

Handwritten signature (X) ▼ _____

7

Certificate will be mailed in window envelope to this address:

Name ▼ _____

Number/Street/Apt ▼ _____

City/State/ZIP ▼ _____

YOU MUST:
• Complete all necessary spaces
• Sign your application in space 7
SEND ALL ELEMENTS IN THE SAME PACKAGE:
1. Application form
2. Nonrefundable filing fee in check or money order payable to Register of Copyrights
MAIL TO:
Library of Congress
Copyright Office
101 Independence Avenue, S.E.
Washington, D.C. 20559-6000

Fees are subject to change. For current fees, check the Copyright Office website at www.copyright.gov, write the Copyright Office, or call (202) 707-3000.

8

Rev: June 2002—20,000   Web Rev: June 2002   ♻ Printed on recycled paper

U.S. Government Printing Office: 2000-461-113/20,021

Copyright
Copyright Office Fee Schedule

effective

The U.S. Copyright Office increased certain fees effective July 1, 2002. These included the fees for—

- renewal registration
- document recordation
- search services
- expedited services
- supplementary registration
- additional certificates

current  fees

Please see the other side of this flyer for a list of Copyright Office fees.

July 1, 2002

Why and How Fees Increased

Effective July 1, 2002, the Copyright Office changed certain fees that it charges for services. Several fees were increased in response to the increased cost of providing services. *However, the basic $30 registration fee was not changed.*

Changes in statutory fees are subject to review by Congress. The Register of Copyrights may change other fees by regulation. Before changing any fees, the Office must first conduct a study of the costs it incurs in providing its services. Fees are adjusted to recover reasonable costs and may include an adjustment to offset inflation. The fees must be fair and equitable. All new fees went into effect on July 1, 2002.

The fee for inspection of Copyright Office records was eliminated effective July 1, 2002.

For further information, consult the Copyright Office website at

www.copyright.gov

Or call the Copyright Public Information Office at (202) 707-3000, 8:30 A.M. to 5:00 P.M. eastern time, Monday through Friday, except federal holidays. The TTY number is (202) 707-6737.

You may write for information to
Library of Congress
Copyright Office
101 Independence Avenue, S.E.
Washington, D.C. 20559-6000

142

⊘ **Copyright Registration Fees**

Effective July 1, 2002

Basic Registrations

Fee to accompany an application and deposit for registration of a claim to copyright

$30 Form TX
$30 Short Form TX
$30 Form VA
$30 Short Form VA
$30 Form PA
$30 Short Form PA
$30 Form SE
$30 Short Form SE
$30 Form SR
$30 Form GATT
—   Form GR/CP (*This form is an adjunct to Forms VA, PA, and TX. There is no additional charge.*)

Renewal Registrations

For works published or registered before January 1, 1978

$60 Form RE
$30 Addendum to Form RE

Group Registrations

Fee to register a group of related claims, where appropriate

$15 Form SE/Group (serials) (*minimum: $45*) (*$/serial issue*)
$55 Form G/DN (daily newspapers and newsletters)
$15 Form GATT/GRP (restored works) (*minimum: $45*) (*$/restored work*)

Supplementary Registrations

Fee to register a correction or amplification to a completed registration

$100 Form CA

Miscellaneous Registrations

$140 Form D-VH (vessel hulls)
$75   Form MW (mask works)

Special Services Related to Registration (Optional Services)

Special Handling for Registration of Qualified Copyright Claims

Fee to expedite processing of qualified claims

$580 Special handling fee (*per claim*)
$50   Additional fee for each (nonspecial handling) claim using the same deposit

Other Fees Associated with Registration

$425 Full-term retention of published copyright deposit
$60   Secure test processing ($/hr)

Appeal Fees (*For claims previously refused registration*)

$200 First appeal
$20   Additional claim in related group (*each*)
$500 Second appeal
$20   Additional claim in related group (*each*)

Other Copyright Service Fees

Recordation of Documents Relating to Copyrighted Works

Fee to make a public record of an assignment of rights or other document

$80   Recordation of a document containing no more than one title
$20   Additional titles (*per group of 10 titles*)
$30   Recordation of NIE containing no more than one title
$1   Additional titles (*each*)
$330 Special handling of recordation of documents

Reference and Bibliography Reports on Copyrighted Works

Fee for searching copyright records and preparing an official report

$75   Preparation of a report from official records ($/hr)
$250 Surcharge for *expedited* Reference and Bibl. reports ($/hr)

Certification and Documents Services: Preparing Copies of Copyright Office Records

Fees for locating, retrieving, and reproducing Copyright Office records

$80   Locating and/or retrieving Copyright Office records ($/hr)
$30   Additional certificate of registration ($/hr)
$80   Certification of Copyright Office records ($/hr)
—   Copying fee: variable depending on format and size
$100 Locating and/or retrieving in-process materials ($/hr)

$200 Surcharge for *Expedited* Certification and Documents Services

Fee of $200/hr for total time spent in fulfilling any or all of these services

—   Locating and/or retrieving in-process records
—   Additional certificate of registration
—   Certification of Copyright Office records
—   Copy of assignment or other recorded document
—   Copy of any other Copyright Office record

Miscellaneous Fees

$10   Receipt for deposit without registration (*Section 407 deposit*)
$30   Online Service Provider Designation
$50   Notice to Libraries and Archives (*each additional title: $20*)
$12   Notice of intention to obtain compulsory license to make and distribute phonorecords

Copyright Office fees are subject to change. For current fees, check the Copyright Office website at *www.copyright.gov*, write the Copyright Office, or call (202) 707-3000.

143

Library of Congress · Copyright Office · 101 Independence Avenue, S.E. · Washington, D.C. 20559-6000 · www.copyright.gov

SL-4: JUNE 2002 — 100,000 WEB REV: JUNE 2002

Trademarks

Trademark Application – Interstate Commerce

PTO Form 1478 (Rev 9/98)
OMB Control #0651-0009 (Exp. 08/31/2004)

Trademark/Service Mark Application

* To the Commissioner for Trademarks *

\<DOCUMENT INFORMATION\>
\<TRADEMARK/SERVICEMARK APPLICATION\>
\<VERSION 1.22\>

\<APPLICANT INFORMATION\>
\<NAME\>   John A. Jones
\<STREET\>   1234 Market Street
\<CITY\>   Anywhere
\<STATE\>   MI
\<COUNTRY\>   USA
\<ZIP/POSTAL CODE\>   22222-3333
\<TELEPHONE NUMBER\>   800-444-5555
\<FAX NUMBER\>   800-444-5550
\<E-MAIL ADDRESS\>   jjones@aol.com
\<AUTHORIZE E-MAIL COMMUNICATION\>   Yes

\<APPLICANT ENTITY INFORMATION\>
\<INDIVIDUAL: COUNTRY OF CITIZENSHIP\>   USA

\<TRADEMARK/SERVICEMARK INFORMATION\>

\<MARK\>   JJPUB

\<TYPED FORM\>   Yes
~ Applicant requests registration of the above-identified trademark/service mark in the United
States Patent and Trademark Office on the Principal Register established by the Act of July 5,
1946 (15 U.S.C. §1051 et seq., as amended). ~

\<BASIS FOR FILING AND GOODS/SERVICES INFORMATION\>
\<USE IN COMMERCE: SECTION 1(a)\>   Yes
~ Applicant is using or is using through a related company the mark in commerce on or in
connection with the below-identified goods/services. (15 U.S.C. §1051(a), as amended.).
Applicant attaches one SPECIMEN for each class showing the mark as used in commerce on
or in connection with any item in the class of listed goods and/or services. ~
\<SPECIMEN DESCRIPTION\>   shipping label; book cover
\<INTERNATIONAL CLASS NUMBER\>   016
\<LISTING OF GOODS AND/OR SERVICES\>   a housemark on a series of fiction and nonfiction
books on a variety of topics
\<FIRST USE ANYWHERE DATE\>   02/09/1999
\<FIRST USE IN COMMERCE DATE\>   06/01/1999

\<FEE INFORMATION\>

<LAW OFFICE INFORMATION>
~ The USPTO is authorized to communicate with the applicant at the below e-mail address ~
<E-MAIL ADDRESS FOR CORRESPONDENCE>   info@jjjjpub.com

<SIGNATURE AND OTHER INFORMATION>
~ **PTO-Application Declaration:** The undersigned, being hereby warned that willful false statements and the like so made are punishable by fine or imprisonment, or both, under 18 U.S.C. §1001, and that such willful false statements may jeopardize the validity of the application or any resulting registration, declares that he/she is properly authorized to execute this application on behalf of the applicant; he/she believes the applicant to be the owner of the trademark/service mark sought to be registered, or, if the application is being filed under 15 U.S.C. §1051(b), he/she believes applicant to be entitled to use such mark in commerce; to the best of his/her knowledge and belief no other person, firm, corporation, or association has the right to use the mark in commerce, either in the identical form thereof or in such near resemblance thereto as to be likely, when used on or in connection with the goods/services of such other person, to cause confusion, or to cause mistake, or to deceive; and that all statements made of his/her own knowledge are true; and that all statements made on information and belief are believed to be true. ~

<SIGNATURE>_____ * please sign here*

<DATE>   _____
<NAME>   John A. Jones
<TITLE>   President

The information collected on this form allows the PTO to determine whether a mark may be registered on the Principal or Supplemental register, and provides notice of an applicant's claim of ownership of the mark. Responses to the request for information are required to obtain the benefit of a registration on the Principal or Supplemental register. 15 U.S.C. §§1051 et seq. and 37 C.F.R. Part 2. All information collected will be made public. Gathering and providing the information will require an estimated 12 or 18 minutes (depending if the application is based on an intent to use the mark in commerce, use of the mark in commerce, or a foreign application or registration). Please direct comments on the time needed to complete this form, and/or suggestions for reducing this burden to the Chief Information Officer, U.S. Patent and Trademark Office, U.S. Department of Commerce, Washington D.C. 20231. Please note that the PTO may not conduct or sponsor a collection of information using a form that does not display a valid OMB control number.

Trademarks

Trademark Application – Intent To Use

Trademark/Service Mark Application

PTO Form 1478 (Rev 9/98)
OMB Control #0651-0009 (Exp. 08/31/2004)

Trademark/Service Mark Application

* To the Commissioner for Trademarks *

\<DOCUMENT INFORMATION>
\<TRADEMARK/SERVICEMARK APPLICATION>
\<VERSION 1.22>

\<APPLICANT INFORMATION>
\<NAME>   JJJJ Publishing, LLC
\<STREET>   1234 Main Street
\<CITY>   Anywhere
\<STATE>   PA
\<COUNTRY>   USA
\<ZIP/POSTAL CODE>   11111-2222
\<TELEPHONE NUMBER>   800-123-4444
\<FAX NUMBER>   800-123-4440
\<E-MAIL ADDRESS>   info@jjjjpub.com
\<AUTHORIZE E-MAIL COMMUNICATION>   Yes

\<APPLICANT ENTITY INFORMATION>
\<OTHER ENTITY TYPE: SPECIFIC NATURE OF ENTITY>   Limited Liability Company
\<STATE/COUNTRY UNDER WHICH ORGANIZED>   USA

\<TRADEMARK/SERVICEMARK INFORMATION>

\<MARK>   JJJJPUB

\<TYPED FORM>   Yes
~ Applicant requests registration of the above-identified trademark/service mark in the United
States Patent and Trademark Office on the Principal Register established by the Act of July 5,
1946 (15 U.S.C. §1051 et seq., as amended). ~

\<BASIS FOR FILING AND GOODS/SERVICES INFORMATION>
\<INTENT TO USE: SECTION 1(b)>   Yes
~ Applicant has a bona fide intention to use or use through a related company the mark in
commerce on or in connection with the below-identified goods/services. (15 U.S.C. §1051(b),
as amended.) ~
\<INTERNATIONAL CLASS NUMBER>   016
\<LISTING OF GOODS AND/OR SERVICES>   A series of fiction and nonfiction books on a variety
of topics.

\<FEE INFORMATION>
\<TOTAL FEES PAID>   325
\<NUMBER OF CLASSES PAID>   1
\<NUMBER OF CLASSES>   1

Trademark/Service Mark Application

<LAW OFFICE INFORMATION>
~ The USPTO is authorized to communicate with the applicant at the below e-mail address ~
<E-MAIL ADDRESS FOR CORRESPONDENCE> info@jjjjpub.com

<SIGNATURE AND OTHER INFORMATION>
~ **PTO-Application Declaration:** The undersigned, being hereby warned that willful false statements and the like so made are punishable by fine or imprisonment, or both, under 18 U.S.C. §1001, and that such willful false statements may jeopardize the validity of the application or any resulting registration, declares that he/she is properly authorized to execute this application on behalf of the applicant; he/she believes the applicant to be the owner of the trademark/service mark sought to be registered, or, if the application is being filed under 15 U.S.C. §1051(b), he/she believes applicant to be entitled to use such mark in commerce; to the best of his/her knowledge and belief no other person, firm, corporation, or association has the right to use the mark in commerce, either in the identical form thereof or in such near resemblance thereto as to be likely, when used on or in connection with the goods/services of such other person, to cause confusion, or to cause mistake, or to deceive; and that all statements made of his/her own knowledge are true; and that all statements made on information and belief are believed to be true. ~

<SIGNATURE>_____ * please sign here*

<DATE>   _____
<NAME> John A. Jones
<TITLE> President

The information collected on this form allows the PTO to determine whether a mark may be registered on the Principal or Supplemental register, and provides notice of an applicant's claim of ownership of the mark. Responses to the request for information are required to obtain the benefit of a registration on the Principal or Supplemental register. 15 U.S.C. §§1051 et seq. and 37 C.F.R. Part 2. All information collected will be made public. Gathering and providing the information will require an estimated 12 or 18 minutes (depending if the application is based on an intent to use the mark in commerce, use of the mark in commerce, or a foreign application or registration). Please direct comments on the time needed to complete this form, and/or suggestions for reducing this burden to the Chief Information Officer, U.S. Patent and Trademark Office, U.S. Department of Commerce, Washington D.C. 20231. Please note that the PTO may not conduct or sponsor a collection of information using a form that does not display a valid OMB control number.

Trademarks

Trademark Application – TEAS

~TRADEMARK/SERVICE MARK APPLICATION (15 U.S.C. §§ 1051, 1126(d)&(e))~

NOTE: The following form complies with the provisions of the Trademark Law Treaty Implementation Act (TLTIA) and the fee increase effective January 10, 2000.

BASIC INSTRUCTIONS

The following form is written in a "scannable" format that will enable the U.S. Patent and Trademark Office (USPTO) to scan paper filings and capture application data automatically using optical character recognition (OCR) technology. Information is to be entered next to identifying data tags, such as <DATE OF FIRST USE IN COMMERCE>. OCR software can be programmed to identify these tags, capture the corresponding data, and transmit this data to the appropriate data fields in the Trademark databases, largely bypassing manual data entry processes.

Please enter the requested information in the blank space that appears to the right of each tagged (< >) element. However, do not enter any information immediately after the section headers (the bolded wording appearing in all capital letters). If you need additional space, first, in the space provided on the form, enter "See attached." Then, please use a separate piece of paper on which you first list the data tag (e.g., <LISTING OF GOODS AND/OR SERVICES>), followed by the relevant information. Some of the information requested *must* be provided. Other information is either required only in certain circumstances, or provided only at your discretion. **Please consult the "Help" section following the form for detailed explanations as to what information should be entered in each blank space.**

To increase the effectiveness of the USPTO scanners, it is recommended that you use a typewriter to complete the form.

For additional information, please see the *Basic Facts about Trademarks* booklet, available at http://www.uspto.gov/web/offices/tac/doc/basic/, or by calling the Trademark Assistance Center, at 703-308-9000. You may also wish to file electronically, from http://www.uspto.gov/teas/index.html.

MAILING INFORMATION

Send the completed form, appropriate fee(s) (made payable to "The Commissioner of Patent and Trademarks"), and any other required materials to:

> Box New App
> Fee
> Assistant Commissioner for Trademarks
> 2900 Crystal Drive
> Arlington, VA 22202-3513

The filing fee for this application is $325.00 *per class* of goods and/or services. You must include at least $325.00 with this application; otherwise the papers and money will be returned to you. Once your application meets the minimum filing date requirements, this processing fee becomes **non-refundable**. This is true even if the USPTO does not issue a registration certificate for this mark.

You may also wish to include a self-addressed stamped postcard with your submission, on which you identify the mark and list each item being submitted (e.g., application, fee, specimen, etc.). We will return this postcard to you, stamped with your assigned serial number, to confirm receipt of your submission.

~TRADEMARK/SERVICE MARK APPLICATION (15 U.S.C. §§ 1051, 1126(d)&(e))~

~To the Assistant Commissioner for Trademarks~
<APPLICANT INFORMATION>

<Name>
<Street>
<City>
<State>
<Country>
<Zip/Postal Code>
<Telephone Number>
<Fax Number>
<e-mail Address>

<APPLICANT ENTITY INFORMATION>~Select only ONE~

<Individual: Country of Citizenship>
<Corporation: State/Country of Incorporation>
<Partnership: State/Country under which Organized>
<Name(s) of General Partner(s) & Citizenship/Incorporation>
<Other Entity Type: Specific Nature of Entity>
<State/Country under which Organized>

<TRADEMARK/SERVICE MARK INFORMATION>

<Mark>
<Typed Form>~Enter YES, if appropriate~
~DISPLAY THE MARK that you want to register on a separate piece of paper (even if simply a word(s)). Please see additional HELP instructions.~

<BASIS FOR FILING AND GOODS/SERVICES INFORMATION>
<Use in Commerce: Section 1(a)>~Applicant is using or is using through a related company the mark in commerce on or in connection with the below-identified goods and/or services (15 U.S.C § 1051(a)).~
<International Class Number(s)>
<Listing of Goods and/or Services>~List in ascending numerical class order. Please see sample in HELP instructions.~

<Date of First Use Anywhere>
<Date of First Use in Commerce>
~Submit one (1) SPECIMEN for each international class showing the mark as used in commerce.~

PTO Form 1478 (REV 12/99)
OMB Control No. 0651-0009 (Exp. 8/31/2001)

U. S. DEPARTMENT OF COMMERCE/Patent and Trademark Office
There is no requirement to respond to this collection of information unless a currently valid OMB number is displayed.

Trademarks

Trademark Application – TEAS

<Intent to Use: Section 1(b)>~*Applicant has a bona fide intention to use or use through a related company the mark in commerce on or in connection with the below-identified goods and/or services (15 U.S.C. § 1051(b)).~*
<International Class Number(s)>
<Listing of Goods and/or Services>~*List in ascending numerical class order. Please see sample in HELP instructions.~*

<Foreign Priority: Section 44(d)>~*Applicant has a bona fide intention to use the mark in commerce on or in connection with the below-identified goods and/or services, and asserts a claim of priority based upon a foreign application in accordance with 15 U.S.C. § 1126(d).~*
<International Class Number(s)>
<Listing of Goods and/or Services>~*List in ascending numerical class order. Please see sample in HELP instructions.~*

<Country of Foreign Filing>
<Foreign Application Number>
<Date of Foreign Filing>

<Foreign Registration: Section 44(e)>~*Applicant has a bona fide intention to use the mark in commerce on or in connection with the below-identified goods and/or services based on registration of the mark in applicant's country of origin.~*
<International Class Number(s)>
<Listing of Goods and/or Services>~*List in ascending numerical class order. Please see sample in HELP instructions.~*

<Country of Foreign Registration>
<Foreign Registration Number>
<Foreign Registration Date>
<Foreign Registration Renewal Date>
<Foreign Registration Expiration Date>
~*Submit foreign registration certificate or a certified copy of the foreign registration, in accordance with 15 U.S.C. §1126(e).~*

150

<FEE INFORMATION>

$325.00 x <Number of Classes>	= <Total Filing Fee Paid>

< SIGNATURE INFORMATION>

~Applicant requests registration of the above-identified mark in the United States Patent and Trademark Office on the Principal Register established by Act of July 5, 1946 (15 U.S.C. § 1051 et seq.) for the above-identified goods and/or services.

The undersigned, being hereby warned that willful false statements and the like so made are punishable by fine or imprisonment, or both, under 18 U.S.C. § 1001, and that such willful false statements may jeopardize the validity of the application or any resulting registration, declares that he/she is properly authorized to execute this application on behalf of the applicant; he/she believes the applicant to be the owner of the trademark/service mark sought to be registered, or, if the application is being filed under 15 U.S.C. § 1051(b), he/she believes applicant to be entitled to use such mark in commerce; to the best of his/her knowledge and belief no other person, firm, corporation, or association has the right to use the mark in commerce, either in the identical form thereof or in such near resemblance thereto as to be likely, when used on or in connection with the goods/services of such other person, to cause confusion, or to cause mistake, or to deceive; and that all statements made of his/her own knowledge are true; and that all statements made on information and belief are believed to be true.~

~Signature~_____

<Date>

<Name>

<Title>

<CONTACT INFORMATION>

<Name>

<Company/Firm Name>

<Street>

<City>

<State>

<Country>

<Zip/Postal Code>

<Telephone Number>

<Fax Number>

<e-Mail Address>

|5|

Trademarks
Declaration of Use   Page 1 of 2

PTO/TM/1583 (Rev 4/2000)
OMB No. 0651-0009 (Exp. 08/31/2004)

* Declaration of Use of Mark Under Section 8 *
* (15 U.S.C. § 1058) *

* To the Commissioner for Trademarks *

<DOCUMENT INFORMATION>
<DECLARATION OF USE OF A MARK UNDER SECTION 8>
<VERSION 1.22>

<TRADEMARK/SERVICEMARK INFORMATION>
<MARK> E-MUSEME.COM
<REGISTRATION NUMBER> 0999999
<SERIAL NUMBER> 72456955
<REGISTRATION DATE> 11/11/1997

<OWNER INFORMATION>
<NAME> E-MUSE ME,LLC
<STREET> 3333 Entertainment Drive
<CITY> Anywhere
<STATE> CA
<COUNTRY> USA
<ZIP/POSTAL CODE> 44444-4444
<E-MAIL ADDRESS> info@emuseme.com

<GOODS AND SERVICES INFORMATION>
<ALL GOODS AND/OR SERVICES IN EXISTING REGISTRATION> Yes

~ The owner is using or is using through a related company the mark in commerce on or in
connection with all the goods/services listed in the existing registration. ~

<FEE INFORMATION>
<SECTION 8 FILING FEE AMOUNT> 100
<NUMBER OF CLASSES> 1
<TOTAL FEES PAID> 100
<NUMBER OF CLASSES> 1

<USE INFORMATION>
<SPECIMEN DESCRIPTION> advertisement

<LAW OFFICE INFORMATION>
<E-MAIL ADDRESS FOR CORRESPONDENCE> info@emuseme.com

~ The USPTO is authorized to communicate with the applicant at the above e-mail address ~

<SIGNATURE AND OTHER INFORMATION>

~ Declaration: The owner is using or is using through a related company the mark in commerce on or in connection with the goods/services identified above, as evidenced by the attached specimen(s) showing the mark as used in commerce. ~

~ The undersigned being hereby warned that willful false statements and the like are punishable by fine or imprisonment, or both, under 18 U.S.C. §1001, and that such willful false statements and the like may jeopardize the validity of this document, declares that he/she is properly authorized to execute this document on behalf of the Owner; and all statements made of his/her own knowledge are true and that all statements made on information and belief are believed to be true. ~

<SIGNATURE>_____ * please sign here*
<DATE> _____
<NAME> Mary C. Jones
<TITLE> President

CERTIFICATE OF MAILING
I hereby certify that this correspondence is being deposited with the United States Postal Service with sufficient postage as first class mail in an envelope addressed to:

Assistant Commissioner for Trademarks
2900 Crystal Drive
Arlington, Virginia 22202-3513

on _____
               Date

_____
               Signature

_____
Typed or printed name of person
signing certificate

Trademarks
Combined Application of Renewal and Declaration of Use   Page 1 of 2

TEAS scannable Form   Page 1 of 2

PTO Form 1963 (Rev 4/2000)
OMB No. 0651-0009 (Exp. 08/31/2004)

* Combined Sections 8 & 9 Declaration/Application *
* (15 U.S.C. §§ 1058 & 1059) *

* To the Commissioner for Trademarks *

<DOCUMENT INFORMATION>
<COMBINED SECTIONS 8 & 9 DECLARATION/APPLICATION>
<VERSION 1.22>

<TRADEMARK/SERVICEMARK INFORMATION>
<MARK> E-MUSEME.COM
<REGISTRATION NUMBER> 0999999
<SERIAL NUMBER> 72456955
<REGISTRATION DATE> 12/01/1993

<OWNER INFORMATION>
<NAME> E-MUSE ME, LLC
<STREET> 3333 Entertainment, Drive
<CITY> Anywhere
<STATE> CA
<COUNTRY> USA
<ZIP/POSTAL CODE> 44444-4444
<E-MAIL ADDRESS> info@emuseme.com

<GOODS AND SERVICES INFORMATION>
<ALL GOODS AND/OR SERVICES IN EXISTING REGISTRATION> Yes

~ The owner is using or is using through a related company the mark in commerce on or in
connection with all the goods/services listed in the existing registration. ~

<FEE INFORMATION>
<COMBINED SECTIONS 8 & 9 FILING FEE AMOUNT> 1000
<NUMBER OF CLASSES> 2
<TOTAL FEES PAID> 1000
<NUMBER OF CLASSES> 2

<USE INFORMATION>
<SPECIMEN DESCRIPTION> brochure
<SPECIMEN DESCRIPTION> advertisement

<LAW OFFICE INFORMATION>
<E-MAIL ADDRESS FOR CORRESPONDENCE> info@emuseme.com

~ The USPTO is authorized to communicate with the applicant at the above e-mail address ~

<SIGNATURE AND OTHER INFORMATION>

TEAS scannable Form   Page 2 of 2

~ *Declaration: The owner is using or is using through a related company the mark in commerce on or in connection with the goods/services identified above, as evidenced by the attached specimen(s) showing the mark as used in commerce.* ~

~ The undersigned being hereby warned that willful false statements and the like are punishable by fine or imprisonment, or both, under 18 U.S.C. §1001, and that such willful false statements and the like may jeopardize the validity of this document, declares that he/she is properly authorized to execute this document on behalf of the Owner; and all statements made of his/her own knowledge are true and that all statements made on information and belief are believed to be true. ~

~ *Declaration: The registrant requests that the registration be renewed for the goods and/or services identified above.* ~

<SIGNATURE>_____ * please sign here*
<DATE>   _____
<NAME> Mary C.Jones
<TITLE> President

CERTIFICATE OF MAILING
I hereby certify that this correspondence is being deposited with the United States Postal Service with sufficient postage as first class mail in an envelope addressed to:

Assistant Commissioner for Trademarks
2900 Crystal Drive
Arlington, Virginia 22202-3513

on _____
                Date

      _____
                Signature

      _____
      Typed or printed name of person
      signing certificate

155

Trademarks
Applicant's Response to Office Action

TRADEMARK

IN THE UNITED STATES PATENT AND TRADEMARK OFFICE

In the Application of
APPLICANT: CASE NO.:
SERIAL NO.:   TRADEMARK LAW OFFICE:
FILED: TRADEMARK ATTORNEY:
MARK:

RESPONSE TO OFFICE ACTION

Box Responses –
Commissioner for Trademarks
2900 Crystal Drive
Arlington, VA 22202-3513

Sir or Madam:

    In response to the Office Action dated _____, please consider the following:

RESPONSE TO REQUIREMENTS

RESPONSE TO REFUSAL

CONCLUSION

    In view of the foregoing, allowance of the above referenced application is respectfully requested.

               Respectfully submitted,

               Telephone: ( )

Dated:_____

Enclosures

PUBLISHING AGREEMENT

THIS AGREEMENT is made this ___ day of _____, 20__ (The "Agreement"), by and between _____, an individual (hereinafter referred to as "Author") located at _____, and ABC Publishing Company, a corporation (hereinafter referred to as "Publisher") whose principal place of business is located at _____, concerning a work presently entitled _____ (as described in greater detail below).

WHEREAS Author seeks to create a book tentatively titled _____ (the "Work");
WHEREAS Publisher seeks to publish the Work; and
WHEREAS both parties agree to be bound by the terms and conditions set forth in this Agreement,

NOW THEREFORE Author and Publisher agree as follows:

1.   Rights Granted. The Author hereby grants, transfers, and assigns to the Publisher the Work for the full term of copyright the exclusive right to publish in hardback and paperback editions (the "Primary Rights") and to sell throughout the world in the English language. The Author also grants and assigns to the Publisher the subsidiary rights to the Work, with exclusive authority to license said rights in all countries and in all languages. The Author hereby reserves all rights not expressly granted to the Publisher.

2.   Delivery and Acceptance of the Manuscript.

     (a)   Author shall deliver to Publisher on or before _____, 20__ (the "Delivery Date"), one (1) original hard copy of the complete Work and one (1) copy on computer disk, together with any supplementary materials (including, without limitation, drawings, illustrations, photographs, maps, graphs, tables). If Author fails to deliver the Work by the Delivery Date, after a thirty (30) day grace period (or such other time period as shall be determined by the Publisher and agreed to in writing by both parties), Publisher may demand the return of all sums paid to or on behalf of Author by Publisher in connection with the Work, and this Agreement shall terminate. Upon termination under these circumstances, Author may not resubmit the Work (or any part thereof) or a similar work to any other publisher without first offering it to Publisher under the same terms contained in this Agreement.

     (b)   Publisher shall inform the Author in writing as to whether the complete Work is acceptable to Publisher in form and content within ninety (90) days of receipt of the complete Work. If Publisher determines the Work is unacceptable but capable of cure, Publisher and Author shall agree upon a time for revision (the "Revision Period") and Publisher shall provide to Author written comments explaining the necessary revisions. If Publisher determines that the first submission cannot be cured or that the revision created during the Revision Period is still unacceptable, Publisher shall have the right, in Publisher's sole discretion, to reject the Work by giving written notice to the

Contracts

Author. If the Work is rejected, Author shall keep fifty percent (50%) of the advances paid to date and shall return the remaining fifty percent (50%) within one year of rejection. The Author may submit the Work to a third party, provided that Author shall remain obligated to repay to Publisher the amounts retained by Author from all proceeds from any sale or license by the Author of rights of any nature in the Work to a third party (the "First Proceeds").

3.   Supplementary Material.

(a)   The Author will prepare, or cause to be prepared, and deliver to the Publisher within ___ weeks of the receipt of page proofs an index to the Work acceptable to the Publisher, unless the parties agree that an index will not be needed.

(b)   If permissions to use copyrighted work in the Work are necessary, the Author shall obtain such permissions at Author's own expense (after consultation with the Publisher) and shall file them with the Publisher at the time the manuscript is delivered (or as agreed to prior to Delivery). Publisher acknowledges that the permissions request form attached hereto as Exhibit A shall be sufficient evidence, when fully and properly executed, of permission.

[NOTE: Attach a copy of the Permissions Request Form]

4.   Representations and Warranties.

(a)   The Author warrants that he/she is the sole owner of the Work and has full power and authority to make this agreement, and that the Work does not infringe the copyright in any other work, violate the rights to privacy or publicity of any person, or constitute a defamation against any person.

(b)   Publisher represents and warrants that it is a company duly organized, validly existing, and in good standing under the laws of its jurisdiction of charter, having all requisite power and authority to enter into this Agreement, and that it will make no additions or changes to the Work that infringe the copyright in any other work, violate the rights to privacy or publicity of any person, or constitute a defamation against any person.

5.   Duty to Publish.

(a)   The Work shall be published by the Publisher in the English language as soon as circumstances permit after acceptance of the completed manuscript, but in no event later than eighteen (18) months after acceptance, at its own expense, in such style or styles and at such price or prices as the Publisher shall deem best suited to the sale of the Work.

(b)   The Author will bear the expense of any alterations made in the proofs by the Author (exclusive of printer's or Publisher's staff errors) which exceed ten percent (10%) of the cost of the composition.

2

6.   Artistic Control. The Publisher, in consultation with the Author, shall make all artistic decisions.

7.   Royalties. The Publisher shall pay to the Author on each copy of the Work sold by the Publisher, the following royalties based on the Net Sales of the Work ("Net Sales" being defined as sales, less returns, at list price less trade discounts):

(a)   Hardback: __% on the first 5,000 copies; __% on the next 5,000 copies; __ on all copies thereafter.

(b)   Paperback: __% on the first 10,000 copies; __% on all copies thereafter.

(c)   Mass Market: __% on the first 150,000 copies; __ % on all copies thereafter.

(d)   On hardback and/or paperback copies sold at special discount of 60% or more from the list price, a royalty of __% of the amount the Publisher receives, except as provided in paragraph 16.

(e)   On hardback and/or paperback copies sold for export (outside the United States and Canada), 75% of the royalties stipulated in paragraphs 8(a) - (c), except as provided in paragraph 16.

(f)   No royalty shall be paid on copies furnished without charge for review, advertising, sample, promotion or other similar purposes, or on damaged copies or Author copies.

[Optional Net Revenue Scheme: The net amount of any compensation received from such dispositions will be divided equally between the Author and the Publisher (after all manufacturing costs, commissions, foreign taxes, and other charges) in lieu of royalty, except that the division of the net proceeds from dramatic, motion picture, and television licenses shall be __% to the Author and __% to the Publisher.]

8.   Subsidiary Rights. The Publisher shall have the sole right to license, sell, or otherwise dispose of the following rights in the Work: publication or sale by book clubs; reprint rights; foreign rights; translation rights; publication in anthologies, compilations, digests, condensations; first and second serial rights (in one or more installments); dramatic, motion picture, and television rights; broadcast by radio; recordings; electronic, mechanical, and visual reproduction; computer programs; microprint, microfiche, and microfilm editions; syndication rights; permission rights (quotations, excerpts, illustrations, etc.); any other rights to the Work not specifically enumerated; and otherwise utilize the Work and material based on the Work.

[NOTE: This is an all-inclusive sub-rights clause and may not be in an author's best interest. A competent professional should carefully and vigorously negotiate this clause.]

159

Contracts

     (e)   [Include provisions for special sub-rights payment schedules not included in (d)]

9.   Accounting and Payments. The Publisher shall render to the Author in June and December of each year a biannual statement of account as of the preceding six (6) month period, which shall signal the close of the preceding accounting period. The statement shall show for that period and cumulatively to date the number of copies (1) printed and bound, (2) sold and returned for each royalty rate, (3) distributed free for publicity purposes, (4) remaindered, destroyed, or lost, as well as the royalties paid to and owed to the Author, and licensing income. Payment shall be made within thirty (30) days of the close of the applicable accounting period in US dollars. If the Publisher sets up a reserve against returns of books, the reserve may only be set up for the four accounting periods following the first publication of the Work and shall in no event exceed fifteen percent (15%) of royalties due to the Author in any period.

10.   Inspection of Books. Author, along with Author's legal or financial representative, shall, upon giving written notice to Publisher or Publisher's designee, have the right once per year to inspect the Publisher's books of account to verify the accounting. If errors in any such accounting are found to be to the Author's disadvantage and represent more than five percent (5%) of the payment to the Author pursuant to said accounting, the cost of the accounting shall be paid by the Publisher. In any case, such payments owed to Author shall be payable immediately.

11.   Copyright. Publisher shall in all versions of the Work published by Publisher under this Agreement, place a notice of copyright in the name of the author (ex: © 2003 by Patsi Pen) in a form and place that Publisher reasonably believes to comply with the requirements of the United States copyright law, and shall apply for registration of such copyright(s) in the name of the Author in the United States Copyright Office. Publisher shall have the right, but not the obligation, to apply for registration of copyright(s) in the Work published by Publisher elsewhere in the world. Author shall execute and deliver to Publisher any and all documents which Publisher deems necessary or appropriate to evidence or effectuate the rights granted in this Agreement, including but not limited to the Instrument of Recordation. Nothing contained in this Section shall be construed as limiting, modifying or otherwise affecting any of the rights granted to Publisher under this Agreement.

12.   Indemnity. Author and Publisher (each an "Indemnifying Party") hereby agree to indemnify and hold each other harmless from and against any and all claims, demands, actions and rights of action (including reasonable attorneys' fees and costs) which shall or may arise by virtue of: (i) anything done or omitted to be done by the Indemnifying Party (through or by his agents, employees or other representatives) outside the scope of, or in breach of the terms of, this Agreement; (ii) any breach of warranty or representation contained herein; and (iii) any misrepresentation, omission or inaccuracy in any schedule, instrument or paper delivered or to be delivered hereunder or in connection with the transaction herein contemplated.

4

13.   Author Copies. The Publisher shall give to the Author, free of charge, ___ copies of each edition of the Work as published. Author may purchase additional copies from Publisher for personal use (not for resale) [alternate clause: which Author may resell, at Author's discretion,] at the best available discount, without royalty to the Author. Publisher may deduct the cost of said additional copies from Author's account in lieu of actual payment by Author for such copies.

14.   Revisions. The Author shall revise the Work (a "Revised Work") ___ times after initial publication and within one (1) year upon the receipt of written request from the Publisher to do so. A Revised Work shall not substantially alter the original Work, and further shall not constitute a new work for [copyright and] royalty escalation purposes. In the event that the Author is unable or unwilling to provide a revision within one (1) year after the Publisher has requested it, or should the Author be deceased, the Publisher may have the revision made at the Publisher's expense (such expense to be recoupable from royalties) [and may display in the revised Work and in advertising the name of the person or persons who perform the revision.]

15.   Out-of-Print, Reversion. If the work goes out of print in all publisher's editions, Author shall have the right to request that Publisher reprint or cause a licensee to reprint the Work. Publisher shall have six (6) months after receipt of any such written request from author to comply, unless prevented from doing so by circumstances beyond Publisher's control. If Publisher declines to reprint the work as described above, or if Publisher agrees to reprint the work but fails to do so within the time allowed, then Author may terminate this Agreement upon thirty (30) days' written notice. Upon such termination, all rights granted under this agreement, except the rights to dispose of existing stock as set forth in paragraph 16 below, shall revert to Author, subject to all rights which may have been granted by Publisher to third parties under this Agreement, and Publisher shall have no further obligations or liabilities to Author except that Author's earned royalties shall be paid when and as due. The work shall not be deemed out of print within the meaning of this section so long as the work is available for sale either from stock in Publisher's, a distributor's or a licensees' warehouse, or in regular sales channels.

[Special clause to address electronic versions of the Work: If Publisher sells no more than _____ copies of Author's Work in either electronic or downloadable format, or by means of print-on-demand technology, over any _____ consecutive month period of this Agreement, then either party may terminate this Agreement upon thirty (30) days' written notice sent to the other party. Upon such termination, all rights granted under this Agreement, except the rights to dispose of existing stock including but not limited to electronic, printed, or audio copies, shall revert to Author, subject to all rights that may have been granted by Publisher to third parties under this Agreement, and Publisher shall have no further obligations or liabilities to Author except that Author's earned royalties shall be paid when and as due.]

161

Contracts

16.   Remaindering. If Publisher shall determine that there is insufficient demand for the Work to enable the Publisher to continue its publication and sale profitably, the Publisher may dispose of the copies remaining on hand as it deems best. In such event, Author shall have the right, within ___ days of receiving written notice from Publisher, to a single purchase of some or all of such copies at the best available discount, and the purchase of film and plates at Publisher's actual cost of manufacture. If Author declines to purchase such copies, Publisher may dispose of such copies, and shall pay Author a sum equal to ten percent (10%) of the amounts actually received by Publisher.

17.   Promotion of the Work. The Publisher may publish or permit others to publish or broadcast without charge and without royalty such excerpts from the Work for publicity purposes as may benefit the sale of the Work. Further, the Author consents to the use of his/her name and likeness to promote and advertise the work; provided such use is dignified and consistent with the Author's reputation.

18.   No-Compete Clause. The Author agrees not to publish or furnish to any other publisher, without the Publisher's written consent, during the term of this agreement any work on the same subject and of the same content and character as the Work covered by this agreement, publication of which would, in the Publisher's opinion, clearly conflict with the sale of the Work.

19.   Options Clause. The Publisher shall, within _____ (__) days from the date of publication, have the option to acquire Author's next book-length work [of [insert genre]] [relating to _____] [on the same terms has set forth hereunder] [on terms to be mutually agreed upon by the parties].

20.   Amendments. The written provisions contained in this agreement constitute the sole and entire agreement made between the Author and the Publisher concerning this Work, and any amendments to this agreement shall not be valid unless made in writing and signed by both parties.

21.   Notice Provisions. Where written notice is required hereunder, such notice, as well as royalty statements and copies of payments to be made hereunder, shall be given or made to the respective party at the addresses in the recitation.

A copy of all notices to Author shall also be sent to:

Author's Agent
Company
Address
Phone:
Fax:
Email:

Author's Attorney
Firm

6

162

Address
Phone:
Fax:
Email:

22.   Arbitration. All disputes arising under this agreement shall be submitted to binding arbitration and shall be settled in accordance with the rules of the American Arbitration Association. Judgment upon the arbitration award may be entered in any court having jurisdiction thereof.

23.   Construction, Governing Law, Binding Effect, and Assignment. This agreement shall be construed and interpreted according to the laws of the State of _____ and shall be binding upon the parties hereto, their heirs, successors, assigns, and personal representatives.

24.   Entire Agreement. This represents the entire agreement between the parties. All modifications must be in writing and signed by both parties.

IN WITNESS WHEREOF, the parties have duly executed this agreement as of the date first written above.

By: [Name of Publisher]

_____
Signatory

_____
Author

_____
Title/Position

_____
Address

_____
Address

_____
City, State Zip

_____
City, State Zip

_____
Social Security Number

163

Contracts

WORK MADE FOR HIRE AGREEMENT
BY AND BETWEEN

_____

AND

_____

THIS AGREEMENT is made by and between _____, a [insert type of entity] located at _____ (hereinafter referred to as "OWNER"), and _____, a [insert type of entity], located at _____ (hereinafter referred to as "you" or "your").

TERMS

This Work-Made-For-Hire Agreement when signed by OWNER and you will confirm the following as our mutual understanding and agreement:

1.   In consideration of the total sum-certain amount of _____ dollars ($_____), you agree to create, provide to and perform for OWNER the specially ordered work and services, referred to below, on a Work-Made-For-Hire basis, as defined under Section 101 of the 1976 Copyright Act, as amended, and on the terms and conditions hereof, to be a supplemental work for OWNER's trade publication, namely [insert title], or for any other uses. All rights of copyright (namely the right to reproduce, to prepare derivative works, to distribute copies, to display the work publicly (or to refrain therefrom), as well as the right of attribution and the right of integrity, and other rights to the specially ordered work and services will vest in OWNER. You obtain no rights of copyright, no right to further compensation, nor any other property or equitable rights in the specially ordered work and services, or in the work in which it is used.

2.   To the extent the rights, including copyright, to the specially ordered work and services do not automatically vest in OWNER, you hereby transfer and assign to OWNER all such rights, including world-wide copyright and renewal rights. Such transfer and assignment is coupled with an interest and is therefore irrevocable. Further, you understand and agree the OWNER reserves the right to terminate your work and services before completion. If so terminated, OWNER will retain all rights to the work as state above, and you shall be entitled to a fair and reasonable portion of the above stated compensation, based upon the amount of work and/or services provided by you to OWNER. You also acknowledge that although it is OWNER's intention to publish _____, to the extent the book is not published and/or released, your supplemental work for the book remains the property of OWNER.

3.   You represent and warrant to OWNER, its successors, designees, licensees and transferees (all hereinafter referred to as "USER") that all items and materials, including without limitation, visual images and designs, writings, dialogue, other copyrightable

works, and ideas, created and provided by you to OWNER hereunder, will not obligate USER to make payment to any other party, nor violated the right of privacy or publicity of any person or party, nor constitute a libel or slander against any person or party, nor infringe upon the trademark, service mark, trade dress, copyright, literary, dramatic, artistic, intellectual, or other legal equitable rights of any person or party. You agree that OWNER may use your name and identity in connection with the work and services, and you shall [shall not] receive credit on all copies of _____ and any promotional materials in which your supplemental works appear.

4.   You understand that the information provided to you, used and created by you, and that which becomes known by you in connection with your work and services for OWNER, which includes ideas, concepts, art, audio-visual, and written materials from which you will be working, is to be treated by you as proprietary, trade secret, and confidential information of OWNER. You warrant you will not discuss or use such information separate of your services rendered, and without OWNER's prior written approval.

5.   This specially ordered work and services you will create and provide to OWNER, which duties you cannot assign are: _____ The due dates for the work and services will be decided upon by mutual agreement in accordance with the publication schedules of OWNER. The due dates set forth and agreed upon are incorporated by reference and made a part of this Agreement.

6.   You agree to return to OWNER or OWNER's designee, all copyrightable works, and elements thereof, information, and materials relating thereto that were provided to you, obtained by you, and that were developed and created hereunder, within twenty-four (24) hours of the last day of work and services, or as otherwise indicated in writing by OWNER or OWNER's designee. Furthermore, you agree to assert no lien against or otherwise cause the materials and rights of OWNER to be encumbered. OWNER's initial designee hereunder is _____, located at _____. Additional or successor designees may be named.

7.   You represent and warrant that you have the full right and authority to enter into this Agreement; you have not made any contract, agreement or commitment in conflict with this Agreement, nor know of any potential conflict that would interfere with or prevent the use of the work and your services; and that you agree to indemnify OWNER and USER for breach of any and all above representations and warranties. You also agree that the warranties made, right obtained, and duty of indemnification shall survive the termination or completion of the work and services under this Agreement. Lastly, you acknowledge that you have been advised that you have the right to seek outside legal counsel and/or advice from your management representative regarding the terms of the Agreement.

Contracts

The undersigned have read, understand and approve this Agreement, and indicate acceptance by signing in the space below.

AGREED AND ACCEPTED:

[OWNER COMPANY]

By: _____

_____
Name

_____
Signature

_____
SSN

_____
Date

COLLABORATION AGREEMENT
BY AND BETWEEN

_____

and

_____

THIS COLLABORATION AGREEMENT ("Agreement") is entered into as of the
_____ day of _____, 20 _____, (the "Effective Date") between
_____, a [enter capacity], located at _____
(hereinafter referred to as "Collaborator 1") and _____, a
[enter capacity], located at _____ (hereinafter referred to as
"Collaborator 2") regarding a project presently titled [insert working title of the
project] ("Work").

TERMS

1.   Description of the Work. The Work shall be approximately _____ words on
the subject of _____.
Materials other than text shall include _____.

[NOTE: Consider attaching a synopsis or outline of the Work and any other
contributions to the Work.]

2.   Term. The term for this Agreement shall be the duration of the copyright,
pursuant to the Copyright Act, in effect on the Effective Date, as extended by any
renewals or extensions thereof (the "Term").

3.   No Agency. The parties to this Agreement are independent of one another,
and nothing contained in this Agreement shall make a partnership, agency, or joint
venture between them.

4.   Collaboration. Each party agrees to cooperate with the other as joint authors
of the Work, to share equally in all tasks and responsibilities as may be necessary to
complete the Work, and to secure its publication and other exploitation, including
research, writing and editing of the Work. However, in order to clarify the respective
duties of each party, the responsibilities shall be divided as follows:

        (a)   Collaborator 1 shall be responsible for [include this collaborator's

                                                                          1

167

Contracts

responsibilities and what, if any, supplementary materials he/she will supply.]

(b)   Collaborator 2 shall be responsible for [include this collaborator's responsibilities and what, if any, supplementary materials he/she will supply.]

(c)   This Agreement shall remain in effect for the duration of the Term (unless otherwise terminated before such time), and shall be binding upon each party's heirs and successors. However, in the event of the death or disability of either party that will prevent completion of his or her respective portion of the Work, or of a revision thereof or a sequel thereto, the other party shall have the right to complete that portion or to hire a third party to complete that portion and shall adjust the authorship credit to reflect the revised authorship arrangements. The deceased or disabled party shall receive payments pursuant to paragraph 5 pro rata to the proportion of his or her work completed or, in the case of a revision or sequel, shall receive payments pursuant to paragraph 5 after deduction for the cost of revising or creating the sequel with respect to his or her portion of the Work. In that case, the active party shall have the sole power to license and contract with respect to the Work, and approval of the personal representative, heirs, or conservator of the deceased or disabled party shall not be required. If all parties are deceased, the respective heirs or personal representatives shall take the place of the parties for all purposes.

(d)   Each party shall complete his or her contribution to the Work by _____, 20 ___, or by the date for delivery of the manuscript as specified in a publishing agreement entered into pursuant to paragraph 12 below (the "Due Date"). In the event either party fails to complete his or her contribution to the Work by the Due Date, subject to subparagraph (c) above, a reasonable extension of time may be agreed to, or, in the alternative, the parties may agree to allow the non-defaulting party to complete the Work as if the defaulting party were deceased or disabled.

5.   Division of Income and Expenses. Income and expenses generated by or on behalf of the Work shall be divided as follows:

(a)   *Division of Income*. Net Income, defined as gross income as reduced by reasonable expenses, shall be divided equally between the parties [or insert other payment provisions] and paid directly to each party (or his or her designee). If either party receives income payable to the other party, the receiving party shall make immediate payment to the other party of such amounts as are due hereunder.

(b)   *Division of Expenses*. Expenses to produce the Work shall be divided equally between the parties [or insert other expense provisions]. Each party shall provide written proof of expenses and maintain a proper accounting of such expenses

2

and corresponding payments. Unless otherwise provided, the parties' expenses shall be reimbursed from the first proceeds received, including but not limited to advances.

6.   Artistic Decisions.

(a)   Each party shall have artistic control over his or her portion of the Work. [Artistic control of the entire Work shall be exercised by _____.]

(b)   The parties shall share ideas and make their work-in-progress available to the other to facilitate completion of the Work. Except as otherwise provided in this Agreement, neither party shall at any time make any changes in the portion of the Work created by the other party without their consent.

7.   Business Decisions.

(a)   All editorial, business and other decisions affecting the Work, which require consent, shall be made jointly by the parties, and no agreement regarding the Work shall be valid without the signatures of both parties. The parties agree to reasonably consult with each other on such matters, and agree not to unreasonably withhold such consent to any decisions or agreements. In the event that the parties cannot mutually agree, the ultimate decision will be made by [_____].

(b)   Each party agrees that any communication by him or her to or from any editor, publisher or other industry professional, including an agent so long as both parties are represented by the same agent, must be promptly provided in a detailed manner by mail, fax, or e-mail to the other party.

8.   Copyright, Trademarks and Other Proprietary Rights.

(a)   The parties agree that the work of each contributor shall be copyrighted in the names of each respective party and that upon completion of each party's contribution, such contributions shall be merged into a joint work with a jointly owned copyright.

(b)   It is further agreed that trademarks, rights in characters, titles, and similar ongoing rights (collectively referred to as "Proprietary Rights") shall be owned jointly and equally by both parties.

9.   Derivative Works.

(a)   No derivative work based on the Work (as defined by the Copyright

3

Contracts

Act, as revised) shall be developed, created or exploited without the equal participation of each party. However, if either party declines to participate in such a derivative work, then the other party shall be free to go forward on his or her own, and the non-participating collaborator shall be entitled to receive out of any Net Income of such derivative works, one-half (1/2) of the amount that would have been payable to the non-participating collaborator if the derivative work had been jointly prepared.

(b)   Material of any and all kinds developed or obtained in the course of creating the work shall be [jointly owned] [the property of the party who developed or obtained it].

10.   Agent. [The parties have entered into an agency agreement with respect to the Work with the following agent:_____.] The parties agree to seek an agency agreement [not to seek an agency agreement]. Any agency contract shall be mutually acceptable to and entered into in the names of and signed by each party, each of whom shall comply with and perform all required contractual obligations.

11.   Publisher; Licenses. [The parties have entered into a publishing agreement with respect to the Work with the following publisher:_____.] The parties agree to seek a publishing agreement [not to seek an publishing agreement]. Any publishing agreement shall be mutually acceptable to and entered into in the names of and signed by each party, each of whom shall comply with and perform all required contractual obligations.

If a mutually agreeable publishing contract for initial publication of the Work is not entered into with a publisher by _____, 20_____, then both parties shall have the option to:

(a)   Jointly self-publish the Work and to enter into a separate publishing agreement to set forth the terms and conditions thereof.

(b)   Terminate this Agreement, pursuant to the procedures set forth in paragraph 13. Each party shall fully inform the other party of all negotiations for such a publishing agreement or with respect to the negotiation of any other licenses or contracts pursuant to this Agreement. The disposition of any right, including the grant of any license, shall require written agreement between both parties. Each party shall receive a copy of any contract, license, or other document relating to this Agreement.

12.   Authorship Credit. The credit line for the Work shall appear as follows wherever authorship credit is given in the Work or in promotion, advertising, or other

4

ancillary uses:_____.

13.   Termination. Except as provided in paragraph 4(c) above, the parties agree to follow the following procedures, if necessary, to terminate this Agreement:

        (a)   If any party withdraws from the collaboration before the final manuscript of the Work is fully completed and accepted for publication for publisher, or, in the case of a self-published Work, if the Work has gone to print (the "Withdrawing Party"), then the rights of the Withdrawing Party (including but not limited to the rights to copyright and financial participation, if any) shall be determined by written agreement signed by all parties, or, if such an agreement cannot be reached, pursuant to the terms of paragraph 16 below.

        (b)   If the parties determine that they are unable, for any reason, to complete the Work despite their best efforts to do so, then they will submit to arbitration as provided in paragraph 16 below, to determine the rights and responsibilities of each party at that time to terminate the collaboration efforts fairly and amicably.

14.   Representations and Warranties; Indemnity. Each party warrants and represents to the other that his or her respective contribution(s) to the Work are original (or that appropriate permissions have been obtained) and do not libel or otherwise violate any right of any person or entity, including but not limited to rights of copyright, publicity, or privacy. Each party indemnifies and holds the other harmless from and against any and all claims, actions, liability, damages, costs, and expenses, including reasonable legal fees and expenses, incurred by the other as a result of the breach of such warranties, representations, and undertakings.

15.   Assignment. This Agreement shall not be assignable by either party hereto, provided, however, that after completion of the Work, either party may assign the right to receive income pursuant to paragraph 5 by giving written notice to the other party.

16.   Arbitration. All disputes arising under this Agreement shall be submitted to confidential binding arbitration and shall be settled in accordance with the rules of the American Arbitration Association. Judgment upon the arbitration award may be entered in any court having jurisdiction thereof.

17.   Jurisdiction. This Agreement shall be governed by the laws of the State of

_____.

18.   Non-Disclosure and Non-Competition.

|71|

5

Contracts

(a)   Each party agrees to hold in trust and confidence all material and information disclosed by one party to the other in connection with the Work, and not to disclose any such material or information to any third party without the prior written consent of the other. All such information and materials shall be regarded as proprietary trade secrets jointly owned and controlled by both parties.

(b)   Each party agrees not to prepare, or to participate in the preparation of, any other work that directly competes with or injures the sales of the Work during the Term without the signed written consent of the other party, such consent not to be unreasonably withheld.

19.   Infringement. In the event of an infringement of the Work, the parties shall have the right to sue jointly for the infringement and, after deducting the expenses of bringing suit, to share equally in any recovery [or insert other recovery provisions]. If either party chooses not to join in the suit, the other party may proceed and, after deducting all the expenses of bringing the suit, any recovery shall be shared between the parties as follows: _____.

20.   Entire Agreement. This Agreement shall be binding upon the parties hereto, their heirs, successors, assigns, and personal representatives. This Agreement constitutes the entire understanding between the parties. Only an instrument in writing signed by both parties can modify its terms. Further, a waiver of any breach of any of the provisions of this Agreement shall not be construed as a continuing waiver of other breaches of the same or other provisions hereof.

21.   Miscellaneous Provisions. Each party shall do all acts and sign all documents required to effectuate this Agreement.

IN WITNESS WHEREOF, the parties hereto have signed this Agreement as of the date first set forth above.

_____	_____
[Collaborator 1]	[Collaborator 2]
SSN: _____	SSN: _____

6

LICENSING AGREEMENT
BY AND BETWEEN

_____

and

_____

THIS LICENSING AGREEMENT is entered into as of the _____ day of
_____, 20 _____, (the Effective Date) between _____, a
[enter capacity], located at _____
(hereinafter referred to as the Licensee) and _____,
a [enter capacity], located at _____(hereinafter referred to as the
Licensor) with respect to the licensing of certain rights in the Licensor s creative
work(s) (hereinafter referred to as the Property).

TERMS

1.   Description of Property. The Licensee wishes to license certain rights in the
Property that the Licensor has created and/or owns and which is described as follows
(as further described in Exhibit A attached hereto):

[NOTE: Be very specific when describing the Property, using title, word count,
subject matter and copyright information or any other information which helps to
identify the Property being licensed with particularity. Also list any other materials
to be provided along with the Property, as well as the form in which it shall be
delivered.]

2.   Delivery Date. The Licensor agrees to deliver the Property on or before
_____, subject to Paragraph 3.

3.   Grant of License. Upon receipt of full payment pursuant to Paragraphs 8 and
9 below, Licensor grants to the Licensee the following [nonexclusive] [exclusive] rights
in the Property: for use as_____ in the _____ language for the
[product] [publication] [purpose] tentatively titled
_____. [For magazine, newspaper or similar contribution:
For one-time North American serial rights].

- 1 -

173

Contracts

4.   Term. The term of this Agreement will begin on the Effective Date and will end one (1) year thereafter. This Agreement will automatically renew each year for an additional term of one (1) year (Automatic Renewal), unless and until either party notifies the other in writing at least thirty (30) days prior to Automatic Renewal that it does not wish to renew this Agreement.

5.   Territory. [Worldwide.] [United States.] [North America.]

6.   Other Limitations. This Agreement shall be limited by the following additional terms: _____.

[EX: if payments to be made hereunder fall to less than $____ for ____ consecutive months, all rights granted will without further notice revert to the Licensor without prejudice to the Licensor s right to retain sums previously paid and collect additional sums due.]

7.   Reservation of Rights. All rights not expressly granted hereunder are reserved to the Licensor, including but not limited to all rights in preliminary and supplementary materials [and all electronic rights. For purposes of this agreement, electronic rights are defined as rights in the digitized form of works that can be encoded, stored, and retrieved from such media as computer disks, CD-ROM, computer databases, and network servers.]

8.   License Fee. Licensee agrees to pay the following fee for the license granted herein:

   A. $_____ [if flat fee — state installment schedule, if any]

   B. an advance of $_____ to be recouped against royalties to be computed as follows [insert royalty schedule]. [if advance against royalties]

9.   Payment Terms. Licensee agrees to pay the Licensor in US currency [insert payment terms (ex: monthly, quarterly, biannually, on the 1st and 15th)]. Overdue payments shall be subject to interest charges of ___ percent (__%) in each month the overdue payment remains outstanding.

10.   [Statements of Account. If there is a royalty schedule]

   A.   The payments due pursuant to Paragraph 8 shall be made by Licensee

- 2 -

174

to Licensor (or Licensor s designee) and shall be accompanied by a statement that includes the amount of and reason for the payment, bank information (if necessary), title and identifying information (ex: ISBN) of the applicable work to which the payment relates, the applicable payment period, and the details of any withholdings for taxes, commissions etc. If Licensee complies with these requirements, Licensor s receipt of the payment shall be a full and valid discharge of the Licensee s obligations hereunder.

B.   Further, Licensee shall render to Licensor a statement of account regarding all revenues received in exploitation of any and all rights granted herein, and all credits and debits relating thereto, and pay to Licensor any amount(s) then owing on the last day of each quarter during the fiscal year beginning January 1 and ending December 31 (March 31, June 30, September 30 and December 31).

11.   Other Uses of Property. If Licensee wishes to make any additional uses of the Property, Licensee shall request permission from the Licensor and make any such payments as are agreed to between the parties at that time.

12.   Alteration of Property. Licensee shall not make or permit any alterations, whether by adding or removing material from the Property, without the permission of the Licensor. Alterations shall be deemed to include the addition of any illustrations, photographs, sound, text, or computerized effects.

13.   Copyright Notice. Copyright notice in the name of the Licensor shall [shall not] accompany the Property and any related advertising and promotional materials when it is reproduced.

14.   Credit. Credit in the name of the Licensor shall [shall not] accompany the Property and any related advertising and promotional materials when it is reproduced.

15.   Indemnification. The Licensee agrees to indemnify and hold harmless the Licensor, and Licensor s affiliates, officers, directors, employees, consultants and agents, against any and all claims, costs, and expenses, including attorney s fees, due to uses for which no release was requested, uses which exceed the uses allowed pursuant to a release, or uses based on alterations not allowed pursuant to Paragraphs 7 and 12.

[Alternate Provision: Licensor and Licensee each indemnify and hold the other

175

- 3 -

Contracts

Licensing Agreement

harmless from and against any and all claims, actions, liability, damages, costs, and expenses, including reasonable legal fees and expenses, incurred by the other as a result of the breach of such warranties, representations, and undertakings.]

16.   Confidentiality.

A.   Confidential Information is defined as information about the disclosing party s business that is proprietary and confidential, which shall include all business, financial, technical and other information of a party marked or designated by such party as "confidential" or "proprietary," or information which, by the nature of the circumstances surrounding the disclosure, ought in good faith to be treated as confidential.

B.   Each party will:

(i) not disclose to any third party or use any Confidential Information disclosed to it by the other except as expressly permitted in this Agreement; and

(ii) take all reasonable measures to maintain the confidentiality of all Confidential Information of the other party in its possession or, which will in no event be less than the measures it uses to maintain the confidentiality of its own information of similar importance.

C.   Notwithstanding the foregoing, each party may disclose Confidential Information as follows:

(i) to the extent required by a court of competent jurisdiction or other governmental authority or otherwise as required by law; or

(ii) on a "need-to-know" basis under an obligation of confidentiality to its legal counsel, accountants, banks and other sources and their advisors.

D.   The terms and conditions of this Agreement will be deemed to be the Confidential Information of each party and will not be disclosed without the written consent of the other party.

- 4 -

176

17.   Termination.

    A.   Either party may terminate this Agreement if the other party materially breaches its obligations hereunder and such breach remains uncured for thirty (30) days following the notice to the breaching party of the breach.

    B.   All payments that have accrued prior to the termination or expiration of this Agreement will be payable in full within thirty (30) days thereof.

    C.   The provisions of this Section 17 (Termination), Section 16 (Confidentiality), Section 15 (Warranty and Indemnity), and Section 18 (Arbitration) will survive any termination or expiration of this Agreement.

18.   Arbitration. All disputes arising under this Agreement shall be submitted to binding arbitration before _____ in the following location _____ and settled in accordance with the rules of the American Arbitration Association. Judgment upon the arbitration award may be entered in any court having jurisdiction thereof. Disputes in which the amount at issue is less than $_____ shall not be subject to this arbitration provision.

19.   Assignment. Neither party may assign this Agreement, in whole or in part, without the other party s written consent (which will not be withheld), except that no such consent will be required in connection with a merger, reorganization or sale of all, or substantially all, of such party s assets. Any attempt to assign this Agreement other than as permitted above will be null and void.

20.   Governing Law. This Agreement shall be governed by the laws of the State of

_____ .

21.   Notice. Any notice under this Agreement will be in writing and delivered to the other party by personal delivery, express courier, confirmed facsimile, confirmed email or certified or registered mail, return receipt requested. Notices will be sent to a party at its address set forth above and as follows:

    Licensor s Attorney

    [Insert information]

177

Contracts

Licensing Agreement

Licensee s Attorney

[Insert information]

22. No Agency. The parties are independent contractors and will have no power or authority to assume or create any obligation or responsibility on behalf of each other. This Agreement will not be construed to create or imply any partnership, agency or joint venture.

23. Severability. Should any provision of this Agreement be void or unenforceable for any reason, such provisions shall be deemed omitted or modified to the extent required by law and this Agreement with such provisions omitted or so modified shall remain in full force and effect.

24. Entire Agreement. This Agreement shall be binding upon the parties hereto, their heirs, successors, assigns, and personal representatives. This Agreement constitutes the entire understanding between the parties. Its terms can be modified only by an instrument in writing signed by both parties. A waiver of a breach of any of the provisions of this Agreement shall not be construed as a continuing waiver of other breaches of the same or other provisions hereof.

IN WITNESS WHEREOF, the parties hereto have signed this Agreement as of the date first set forth above.

ACCEPTED AND AGREED TO:

[Licensor]   [Licensee]

_____   _____

PERMISSION REQUEST FORM

The Undersigned hereby grants permission to _____,
(hereinafter referred to as the Author), located at _____, and
to the Author s successors and assigns, to use the material specified in this
Permission Form (hereinafter referred to a Material) in the book titled
_____ (the Work) to be published by
_____.

1.   The Material.

     A.   Title and/or nature of Material: [Insert].

     B.   Exact description of Material: [Insert].

     C.   Source of the Material: [Insert].

2.   Publication Information.

     A.   The Material has [has not] been previously published.

     B.   [If published, include copyright notice and ownership information.]

3.   Grant of Rights. Author, or Author s designees, shall have the irrevocable right
to use the Material in the Work and in any future revisions, editions, and electronic
versions thereof, including nonexclusive world rights in all languages. It is understood
that the grant of this permission shall in no way restrict republication of the Material
by the Undersigned or others authorized by the Undersigned.

[Alternate Clause: Grant of Rights Author, or Author s designees, shall have the
exclusive and irrevocable right to use the Material in the Work and in any future
revisions, editions, and electronic versions thereof, including nonexclusive world rights
in all languages.]

4.   Copyright Notice and Credit.   The Material shall be accompanied on
publication by a copyright notice as follows:
_____ and a credit line as follows: The
_____ is reproduced from [inert name/description of material],
by _____ [date]. Used with the permission of the [publisher/author],
_____.

5.   Miscellaneous Provisions. [Insert other provisions, if any:

Page 1 of 2

179

Contracts

_____.]

6.   Ownership.   The Undersigned warrants that he/she has the exclusive right to
grant permission to use the Material.

[Alternate insert: The Undersigned does not have the exclusive right to permit use of
the Material and permission must also be granted by the following owners:
_____.]

AGREED TO AND ACCEPTED:

_____   _____
[Name]   Date
Business Name: _____

Business Address:
_____

City, State Zip:
_____

Business Telephone _____   Fax: _____

E-mail _____ Website: _____

180

Glossary

acceptance A publisher's approval of a delivered manuscript (or other item to be delivered).

author Generally a writer, but in the context of the Copyright Act, it includes anyone who creates an original work.

attribution, right of Ensures that artists are properly identified with the works of art they create and that they are not identified with works they did not create.

automated database A body of facts, data, or other information assembled into an organized format suitable for use in a computer and comprising one or more files.

Berne Convention An international copyright treaty that requires all signatories to eliminate formality requirements as a condition to copyright protection. But the formality requirements eliminated by amendment remain important because works created after 1978, the enactment date of the act of 1976, but before 1989, when the act of 1976 was revised and when the United States signed the Berne Convention, are governed by the first version of the 1976 act.

collaboration agreement An agreement between two or more people who contribute work to a book or other creation.

collective works Defined in the Copyright Act as "a number of contributions, constituting separate and independent works in themselves . . . assembled into a collective whole." Individuals or entities who combine individual contributions into one collection hold the copyright in the collection as a whole. But the individual authors retain rights to the individual work apart from the collection. This limitation is found in section 201(c) of the Copyright Act: "In the absence of an express transfer of the copyright or of any rights under it, the owner of the copyright in the collective work is presumed to have acquired only the privilege of reproducing and distributing the contribution as part of that particular collective work, any revision of that collective work, and any later collective work in the same series." Thus, other than the rights to reproduce and distribute the collection, and the right to create a derivative work of the collection, the individual contributors to the collection retain the copyright to their individual contributions.

common law A body of law that is made up of cases rather than laws enacted by legislation.

consideration A legal concept best described as the benefit or detriment that induces someone to make a promise and enter into a contractual arrangement based on the terms, conditions, rights, and obligations agreed to by the parties involved.

copies According to the Copyright Act, material objects, other than phonorecords, in which a work is fixed by any method now known or later developed, and from which the work can be perceived, reproduced, or otherwise communicated, either directly or with the aid of a machine or device. The term "copies" includes the material object, other than a phonorecord, in which the work is first fixed.

copyleft A play on the word "copyright" used by a few people who have created a movement to oppose what they deem to be an unfair monopoly on creative expression held by copyright owners, particularly in the software industry. This term is not found in the Copyright Act itself. Rather, it was created to challenge established copyright laws. "Copyleft" is used primarily by members of the Free Software Foundation, which promotes GNU, a project designed to provide software that is free from licensing fees or restrictions on use. Richard Stallman started the GNU project in 1983 based on his belief that software should contain a notice and a General Public License that grants reuse and reproduction rights to everyone and requires anyone who uses it to grant the same rights to others.

copyright The exclusive rights of a copyright owner on a work to make and distribute copies, prepare derivative works, and perform and display the work publicly.

copyright registration Submitting the copyrighted work to the Copyright Office, pursuant to the rules and guidelines set forth by that office.

created When a work is fixed in a copy or phonorecord for the first time. When a work is prepared over a period of time, the portion of it that has been fixed at any particular time constitutes the work as of that time; and when the work has been prepared in different versions, each version constitutes a separate work.

damages Generally, a sum of money paid in compensation for loss or injury.

delivery The act of giving the manuscript (or other item to be delivered) to the publisher.

delivery date The stipulated date by which an author must deliver the manuscript to the publisher.

deposit The physical copy or copies that must be submitted along with a copyright registration form.

execute To complete, make valid, or give effect by signing.

first proceeds The money received by an author from any sale or license of any rights in his or her copyrighted work to a third party (someone other than the company that originally agreed to publish the work). This situation may arise if the publisher and author enter into a publishing contract, the publisher pays the author an advance, and later the publisher rejects the author's manuscript. If the author then sells the work to another publisher, the first publisher may require the author to repay it from the first money payable to the author as a result of the second publishing deal.

independent contractor One who is self-employed and has the right to control the means and methods of performing work.

integrity, right of Allows a visual artist to protect his or her work from modifications or destruction that injures the artist's reputation.

Inter-American Convention for Trademarks and Commercial Protection A treaty between the United States and certain Latin American countries that are not members of the Paris Convention.

joint work A work prepared by two or more authors with the intention that their contributions be merged into inseparable or interdependent parts of a unitary whole.

Lanham Act The federal law that provides for the registration of trademarks and establishes a system for the administration of the Patent and Trademark Office.

legal vetting See vetting.

legalese Expressions used primarily by lawyers to articulate and discuss legal issues.

licensing agreement An agreement that sets forth the terms that allow others the limited right to use your work (or for you to use the work of others).

literary works Works, other than audiovisual works, expressed in words, numbers, or other verbal or numerical symbols or indicia, regardless of the nature of the material objects, such as books, periodicals, manuscripts, phonorecords, film, tapes, disks, or cards, in which they are embodied.

Madrid Agreement A treaty that provides for the international registration of trademarks. It was adopted in 1891 at a conference held in Madrid, Spain, and is administered by WIPO (www.wipo.org). It is augmented by the Madrid Protocol, another treaty for the international registration of trademarks.

Madrid Union The organization of all the countries that belong to the Madrid Agreement, which allows trademark owners in member countries to file for registration in any member country by filing a single standardized application.

184

moral rights Refers collectively to the right of attribution and the right of integrity.

Paris Convention A treaty relating to trademarks and other intellectual property, which has 140 members countries including the United States. Each member country guarantees to the citizens of the other countries the same rights in trademark matters that it gives to its own citizens.

phonorecords Material objects on which sounds are recorded, such as cassette tapes, CDs, or LPs – but not soundtracks for motion pictures or other audiovisual works.

primary rights The main set of rights that a publisher intends to exploit. Generally this means the right to publish the work in book form (hard cover and/or paperback rights, and perhaps book club rights and so forth). Compare with subsidiary rights below.

publication The distribution of copies or phonorecords of a work to the public by sale or other transfer of ownership, or by rental, lease, or lending. The offering to distribute copies or phonorecords to a group of persons for purposes of further distribution, public performance, or public display constitutes publication. A public performance or display of a work does not of itself constitute publication.

public domain The total absence of copyright protection in a work. A work in the public domain is available to anyone to copy it, distribute it, perform it, display it, make derivatives of it, or use it as he or she sees fit. The author of a work in public domain has none of the exclusive rights that apply to a copyrighted work. Note that the public domain is not an actual place or database but a term that describes the absence of copyright protection. Furthermore, it does not refer to freeware or shareware. In actuality, free- and shareware are copyrighted software distributed without advance payment.

publisher A person or entity that produces any periodical, magazine, newspaper, book, manual, advertising materials, or other similar material, whether in printed, electronic, or other form.

revision period The period of time a publisher grants to an author to revise a manuscript.

185

subsidiary rights The secondary set of rights that may be transferred to a publisher. This may include rights that exist as a result of the primary rights, for example, audio, motion picture and TV, dramatic, mass market paperback, and electronic rights. Compare with primary rights above.

vetting A line-by-line review of a manuscript for potential legal issues.

References

Books

Copyright Law Reporter and *Copyright Law Decisions*. Riverwood, IL: CCH Incorporated, 1978. These companion books focus on cases and analysis, and are geared toward experienced copyright and intellectual property practitioners.

Goldstein, Paul. *Copyright*. New York: Aspen Law & Business, 1996. This four-volume treatise explains fundamental copyright law in a way that non-specialists can understand.

Guinn, David, and Harold Orenstein. *Entertainment Law & Business: A Guide to the Law and Business Practices of the Entertainment Industry*. Vol. 2. Salem, New Hampshire: Butterworth Legal Publishers, 1989.

Kirsch, Jonathan. *Kirsch's Handbook of Publishing Law*. Venice, CA: Acrobat Books, 1995.

Nimmer, Melville B. *Nimmer on Copyright*. New York: Matthew Bender, 1976. Considered by intellectual property practitioners and judges to be the leading treatise on copyright, this ten-volume set covers every conceivable aspect of copyright law. Not appropriate for non-lawyers.

Stephen, Laura Lee, ed. *The E-Copyright Law Handbook*. New York: Aspen Law & Business, 2002.

Articles

Moore, Schuyler M. "Raising Defenses to Right-of-Publicity Claims." Parts 1 and 2. *Entertainment Law & Finance* 17, no. 6 (2001): 3–4; no. 7 (2001): 3–4.

Web Sites

Legal Information Institute of Cornell University:

Contracts	www.law.cornell.edu/topics/contracts.html
Copyright	www.law.cornell.edu/topics/copyright.html
Damages	www.law.cornell.edu/topics/damages.html
Patent	www.law.cornell.edu/topics/patent.html
Publicity	www.law.cornell.edu/topics/publicity.html
Trademark	www.law.cornell.edu/topics/trademark.html
Unfair Comp	www.law.cornell.edu/topics/unfair_competition.html

www.Freeadvice.com

www.FindLaw.com

www.authorsguild.org

www.copyright.gov

www.uspto.gov

www.wipo.org

www.icann.org

About the Authors

Tonya M. Evans, Esquire, also known as Lawyer by day, Poet by night™, is an attorney at the Philadelphia law firm of Evans & Borden Evans, LLC. She practices in the areas of intellectual property (copyright, trademark, licensing), entertainment law (publishing, music), and estate planning (wills, trusts). Tonya and her law partner, Susan Borden Evans, who is also her mother, have developed a professional niche within the publishing industry, representing authors in the review and negotiation of publishing and subsidiary rights deals, and educating authors through seminars and workshops on self-publishing and literary law.

Tonya received a B.S. in communication studies from Northwestern University, which she attended on a full four-year tennis scholarship. Thereafter, she played on the women's professional tennis tour for four years, competing most notably at the U.S. Open and Virginia Slims of Philadelphia in 1993.

In 1995, Tonya attended Howard University School of Law. She served as editor-in-chief of the Howard Law Journal and graduated with honors in 1998. She served as law clerk to Judge Theodore McKee in the Third Circuit Court of Appeals and worked at large law firms before joining practice with her mother. Tonya is a member of the Pennsylvania, New Jersey, District of Columbia, Eastern District of Pennsylvania, and Third Circuit Bars.

Tonya lectures across the country on copyright and trademark law, and on self-publishing and successful negotiations in the publishing industry. She has also contributed to *Black Issues Book Review* and *QBR: The Black Book Review*. In addition, she is an accomplished poet, performer, and writer. Her books include *And Then One Day She Knew*, *Seasons of Her*, and *SHINE!*

Susan Borden Evans, Esquire, received her B.S. from Howard University, with a major in chemistry and a minor in related sciences, and her M.Ed. and J.D. from Temple University. Susan is an intellectual property attorney in the Philadelphia firm of Evans & Borden Evans, LLC. She concentrates her practice in patent and trademark prosecution, and contract review and negotiation. Susan has successfully negotiated publishing agreements and licensing and sub-licensing agreements, and she has prosecuted hundreds of patent applications.

She is a former chairperson of the Intellectual Property Committee of the Philadelphia Bar Association and a former president of the Barristers Association of Philadelphia. Susan lectures regularly across the country on aspects of intellectual property and publishing law, and is a member of the Pennsylvania Bar and the Patent Bar.

Acknowledgments

First, we give honor to our Creator for blessing us with the time, talents, patience, and courage to make our dreams a reality.

Much appreciation goes to the Borden family. They nurture us, sustain us, tolerate us, love us, and are always there for us – especially Nana, Billy, Carol, Johnny, John Jr., Tré, Brittany, and Lin. Our thanks also to the Evans family – and especially Tonya's father, Dr. Richard A. Evans, who always provides her with important words of wisdom. And, for their unconditional love and support, we thank our wonderful new family: Tonya's husband, Orville Russel Walls III, and Dr. and Mrs. Orville Russel Walls Jr., Kathleen, and Brian.

We thank Sandi, Ruby, and Sheila, the inner circle "Bs" Diane, Covette, Barbara, and Robin, the bridesmaid crew, and Carla Waddles, a screenwriter and Tonya's soul sister, for being our dearest sisterfriends.

Dan Poynter, the publishing guru, went above and beyond the call of duty to help us help ourselves. We deeply appreciate his assistance, encouragement, advice, and leadership.

We thank Tia Shabazz and the members of Black Writers Alliance (www.black-writers.org), especially Brian Egeston, Monica Blache, Jamellah Ellis, and Pat G'Orge-Walker, for their guidance and support from the very beginning of our literary journey. Thanks to *Black Issues Book Review*, particularly Mondella Jones, QBR's Max Rodriguez and Nancey Flowers, *Foreword Magazine*'s Stacy Price and Victoria Sutherland, for helping us spread the word about FYOS and our work. To Tracy Price-Thompson, C. Kelly Robinson, Kwame Alexander, Travis Hunter, Denise Turney, Leslie Esdaile, Karen E. Quinones-Miller, and the rest of our writer family, many thanks for being our literary mentors and lifeline.

With deep appreciation we thank our editor, Lisa A. Smith. Her professionalism and the quality of her work are second to none. We feel privileged to have her on our team because, with her insight and ability, she has helped us transform our idea into a book that far exceeded our expectations. And thanks to James "True" Jones for an amazing cover design. He listened to our nebulous concepts and turned them (almost overnight) into a first-rate cover that pops.

For their support, we are grateful to Melody Guy, Chris Jackson, John McGregor, and those seminar presenters not already mentioned and to book clubs and independent bookstores, including Basic Black Books, It's a Mystery to Me, Robin's Books, Ligorious Books, Hakim's Bookstore, Al-Furqan Bookstore, and Black Images Book Bazaar owned by Emma Rodgers.

To all who did not support our endeavors in the beginning, our gratitude because they strengthened our resolve to tap into our inner selves. To those who did support us (both named and unnamed), many, many thanks because they made us even stronger by reminding us why we do what we do.

And last but not least, thanks to Clarissa Pinkola Estes, who, in her book *Women Who Run With the Wolves*, advised that "all that you are seeking is also seeking you."

Index

195

W

Books Published by FYOS Entertainment, LLC

Under the FYOS™ Publishing Imprint

Poetry

- *Seasons of Her: A Collection of Poetry*
- *SHINE!* Inspirational Poetry
  w/Companion CD
- *An Old Soul Reborn*
- *Desire True*

Fiction

- *And Then One Day She Knew*
- *The Blues*

Under the LE Series™ Books Imprint

Reference Guides for Authors

- *Literary Law Guide for Authors:
  Copyright, Trademark, and Contracts
  in Plain Language*

About the Publisher

FYOS™ Entertainment, LLC, is an independent publisher of law-related topics, poetry, and fiction. FYOS™ also offers a wide range of literary services and events for authors and poets.

The Literary Entrepreneur Affiliate Program™ (also called LEAP™)

A dynamic author-assistance service that lets authors retain their rights while allowing an industry professional to showcase and promote their work directly from FYOS.com and LEAPMembers.com, and via nationally distributed newsletters and targeted mail.

FYOS offers a range of services including

- Promotion
- National distribution and exposure
- Title showcases at conferences and other literary events
- Member Web pages
- Order fulfillment
- Secure credit card processing
- Writers' resources
- Discounts on seminars and other services
- Memberships beginning at ONLY $25 per month

Visit www.LEAPMembers.com for more information.

FYOS™ Seminar Series

FYOS assembles leading industry professionals to offer affordable quarterly seminars on topics of interest to writers. Past seminars have included "Demystifying Literary Law," "New Technologies in the Literary Industry," and "Successful Self-Publishing for the Literary Entrepreneur."

Visit www.FYOS.com/seminars.htm for more information.

The Find Your Own Shine® Newsletter

This free newsletter provides information for the poet, writer, and Literary Entrepreneur. The content of the newsletter, sent via e-mail or regular mail, encourages you to tap into your greatness through the written and spoken word. The content includes information about seminars, publications, and events, and provides valuable resources.

Subscribe to the Find Your Own Shine® newsletter at www.fyos.com.

About Evans & Borden Evans, LLC

The attorneys at EBE Law counsel clients throughout the United States in the areas of intellectual property, publishing law, business law, and estate planning.

EBE Law is a twenty-first century firm whose attorneys use cutting-edge technology to streamline the delivery of their services and to increase quality and efficiency. Their aim is to create a partnership with their clients, their community, and their profession. They are committed to client confidentiality, accessibility, and the highest degree of professional responsibility.

EBE Law News™ – An Online Newsletter

The law is constantly being developed, revised, and changed. EBE Law provides a free, subscription-only, online newsletter, titled EBE Law News™, to keep you informed about the latest developments, cases, and trends that affect the publishing industry and entrepreneurs. Subscriber information is kept strictly confidential and is never loaned or sold to third parties.

Contact the attorneys at Evans & Borden Evans, LLC, for a consultation or to sign up for EBE Law News™.

By Mail	By E-mail or Web	By Phone	By Fax
2043 Walnut Street Suite 2000 Phila. PA 19103	info@ebelaw.net www.ebelaw.net	215-972-8001	215-972-8076

Register Right™ Copyright Registration Service

If you don't want to be bothered with the details, let Register Right™ register your work on your behalf for a reasonable fee. The experienced attorneys at Evans & Borden Evans, LLC, will

- streamline your registration process
- select the right form for your work
- properly format your forms and ensure that all required documentation, information, and work deposits are submitted in a timely, professional, and complete manner
- deliver up-to-the-minute, detailed information when your copyright registration is pending
- send you your official registration certificate when the process is complete

Of course, this is nothing that you couldn't do on your own. But letting experienced attorneys do it for you will save you time, give you peace of mind, and allow you to concentrate on writing. Find out more at www.ebelaw.net.

The Register Right™ fee is only $85.95 and includes

- Copyright Office registration fee ($30.00)
- Postage and handling ($15.95)
- Service charge ($40.00)
- NO HIDDEN CHARGES

By Mail	By E-mail or Web	By Phone	By Fax
2043 Walnut Street Suite 2000 Phila. PA 19103	info@ebelaw.net www.ebelaw.net	215-972-8001	215-972-8076

In Future Editions and Publications from

LE Series™ Books
(An imprint of FYOS Entertainment, LLC)

 *Literary Entrepreneur Series™*

- Case law and legislation updates
- Hot topics in intellectual property (copyright vs. copymonopoly)
- Expanded section on subsidiary rights
- Revised and new forms
- Author Q&A
- A special section for self-published authors
- Expanded commentary for forms
- A special section for freelance writers
- *International Law and the Author*
- *Internet and Electronic Publishing Law*

If you have a topic you'd like to see covered in a future edition, e-mail your question, comment, or topic to literarylaw@hotmail.com or visit www.literarylawguide.com.